They Call Him Pastor

They Call Him Pastor

Married Men in Charge
of Catholic Parishes

Ruth A. Wallace

Foreword by Bishop Richard J. Sklba

Paulist Press
New York/Mahwah, N.J.

Cover design by Tim McKeen

Book design by Lynn Else

Library of Congress Cataloging-in-Publication Data

Wallace, Ruth A.
    They call him pastor : married men in charge of Catholic parishes / Ruth A. Wallace.
        p.   cm.
    Includes bibliographical references and index.
    ISBN 0-8091-4171-X (alk. paper)
    1. Lay ministry—Catholic Church.   2. Men in church work—Catholic Church.   3. Married people in church work—United States.   4. Spouses of Clergy—United States.   5. Children of clergy—United States.   6. Catholic Church—United States—Clergy. I. Title.
BX1916 .W35 2003
262′.15273—dc21

                                                                    2003005783

Published by Paulist Press
997 Macarthur Boulevard
Mahwah, New Jersey 07430

www.paulistpress.com

Printed and bound in the United States of America

Contents

DEDICATION

*In memory of Bishop Raymond A. Lucker,
the first diocesan bishop to bring this new
form of leadership into Roman Catholic parishes
in the United States*

Foreword

When the Roman Congregation for Divine Worship promulgated the *Directory for Sunday Celebrations in the Absence of a Priest* on June 2, 1988,[1] they were recognizing a profound pastoral and sacramental need in the Church today. They were also legitimating one of the temporary remedies already in existence in various dioceses and nations throughout the world. It was a serious moment of awareness and recognition.

In the United States, as in other parts of the Catholic world, the declining number of ordained priests had resulted in a corresponding increase in the number of parish communities without resident pastors. This in turn led to the appointment of other ministers, including qualified laity, to serve that role, at least in the day-to-day pastoral needs of any contemporary parish.

In a sense, the dioceses of our country discovered that they had reverted by necessity to earlier times of missionary settlement, when local communities attempted to organize their religious communal lives under lay leadership while awaiting the periodic visit of a priest for the celebration of the sacraments.

The primary difference, of course, can be found in the fact that today's local lay leader is inevitably more qualified by theological and pastoral study, and usually occupied in a full-time appointment to this work. Moreover, the parish community itself is not in a state of being newly established but rather very stable, having been served by a series of ordained clergy over many decades.

First, in her 1992 pioneering study entitled *They Call Her Pastor: A New Role For Catholic Women*,[2] Dr. Ruth Wallace of George Washington University in Washington, D.C., explored the phenomenon of women appointed to provide pastoral leadership for Roman Catholic congregations in the United States. At a time when the emerging leadership of women was being encouraged

1

throughout all of society, and against the historical background of strong women religious who had exercised superb ministry in educational and health care fields, the entrance of women into pastoral leadership merited close professional study and analysis. That volume offered abundant insights.

Now, some ten years later, Dr. Wallace has gathered a great deal of information on the phenomenon of married men appointed to that same pastoral responsibility. This precise focus clearly has some slightly different implications. Countless interviews with the men themselves, their wives and children, as well as the parishioners they serve, offer a fascinating insight into this model of pastoral care for parishes without resident priest pastors.

For over a millennium the discipline of Western Catholicism has insisted on celibacy as a condition and constant characteristic for ordained ministry. Moreover, in the United States with its history of separation of Church and State, each parish community developed its own corporate structure with a convergence of pastoral and legal authority in the person of the priest pastor. The blessing of that structure was an inner cohesion and blending of sacramental life and mission. The independence and at times isolation of parish communities during the great ethnic migrations of the past century and a half reinforced that concentration of authority and responsibility on the person of the pastor alone. With the clear call of the Second Vatican Council for greater lay involvement in the life and ministry of the Church, a new era had dawned.

The parish director/pastoral administrator model of leadership, which was shared between the local lay leader and the visiting sacramental priest, has often been able to provide a double set of gifts to any parish served by that structure. This is particularly true when the personalities of the team are chosen carefully for compatibility, flexibility, and complementarity of pastoral skills.

At the same time, the division could separate liturgy from the true life of the parish community. In light of our strong

Catholic sacramental tradition, I probably would personally prefer to maintain the unity of sacramental life and pastoral leadership. This would require, however, a change in the discipline of ordained ministry in Western Catholicism. I would endorse thoughtful reflection on this model for whatever wisdom it might contribute toward that discussion in the Church.

The unique challenges for wives and children in this model of lay pastoral leadership, however, deserve the greatest of careful attention. High expectations, public scrutiny, and the struggle to respect the individual interests and profession of a wife can make the model very stressful. The need to establish a healthy balance of life and ministry is a constant effort for any pastor. The increase of persons affected makes such boundaries even more important as the following chapters illustrate so compellingly.

I concluded my study of this volume convinced that a uniform terminology and common job description for this model would be a blessing for everyone. Most of all, however, the studies of Dr. Wallace, with all their anecdotal enrichment, have enabled me to appreciate the hard and dedicated work of these men together with their wives and families even more than ever! I salute her for this professional contribution to the life of the Church today.

Bishop Richard J. Sklba
Auxiliary Bishop of Milwaukee

Preface

This book is the result of my visits to twenty parishes throughout the United States where the diocesan bishop appointed a married man as the parish leader. It reveals the thoughts, feelings, and strategies of the principal actors in each of these parishes: the married man in charge of the parish, his wife, their children, the parishioners, the visiting priest serving as sacramental minister, and the bishop. Although their names will not appear in these pages, I am forever in their debt for the gift of their time and their kindness and encouragement before, during, and after my visits to these parishes.

I have spent the better part of almost seven years working on this research project. Thanks to a summer research grant from the George Washington University Facilitating Fund, I was able to conduct an exploratory study in the summer of 1995 that provided the focus for this research project. I would like to thank the Lilly Endowment for a grant that provided the time and resources for my travels throughout the United States for the collection of data in 1996–97. I am also grateful to the Louisville Institute for a grant that provided a research leave in the fall semester of 2001 for the final writing stage, and to the dean of the College of Arts and Sciences at George Washington University for a reduction of my teaching load during the spring semester of 2001.

In addition to my family and my undergraduate and graduate students who lived through the various stages of this study with me, there were many personal friends and colleagues who helped me at various stages of this project. In particular, I want to thank Bonnie Brennan, John Coleman, James Coriden, Charles Curran, Sally Davis, Helen Rose Ebaugh, Susan Farrell, Brian Froehle, Mary Gautier, Thomas Green, Shirley Hartley, Fred Hofheinz, Dean Hoge, Carla Howery, Helen Kelley, Fred Kniss,

Donald Lehman, Edward Lehman, James Lewis, Patrick McNamara, Martin Mangan, Frank Maurovich, Katherine Meyer, Loretta Morris, Philip Murnion, Paula Nesbitt, James Provost, Kay Sheskaitis, William Silverman, Thomas Sweetser, and my colleagues in the Sociology Department at George Washington University.

Chapter 1
Introduction

Over the past twelve years I have been working on parish research projects that may seem as improbable as Dorothy's travels in *The Wizard of Oz*. During 1989–90 I traveled to twenty parishes throughout the United States where the people in charge were sisters (members of religious communities) and married women.[1] In 1996–97 I traveled to twenty parishes where the people in charge were married deacons and married laymen. This book reports the findings from my second research project on new forms of parish leadership.

When they talk about their pastors or read about parish leaders, Catholics tend to think "ordained priest." This is especially true if they live in dioceses where at least one priest resides in every parish. Imagine, then, the reaction of a Catholic on vacation who rings a rectory doorbell, and the teenaged boy who opens the door, answers a question about Sunday Masses and then proudly announces, "My dad's the one in charge here!" The fact that some Catholic parishes have been entrusted to the care of married men may seem strange to many Catholics, because it contradicts their own parish experience.

Church Law and Key Terms

The change in church law that opened the door in 1983 for alternate parish leadership is canon 517.2 of the *Code of Canon Law*. The canon provides that when there is a shortage of priests, a diocesan bishop may entrust the pastoral care of a parish to "a deacon" or "to another person who is not a priest."[2]

Two key terms that will be used often in this book are *parish* and *pastor*. A parish is described in canon 515.1 of the *Code of*

Canon Law, as "a certain community of the Christian faithful sta-
bly constituted in a particular church, whose pastoral care is
entrusted to a pastor *(parochus)* as its proper pastor *(pastor)* under
the authority of the diocesan bishop." Most parishes are territo-
rial in that their members include all Catholics living within a certain geographic location. But parishes can also be established
based on nationality, language, rite, or other factors, like affiliation with a university or a military base.[3]

A list of the activities of a parish community in the new *Code
of Canon Law* include the following: (1) proclamation of the word
of God, preaching, teaching, Catholic education of adults and
children; (2) worship of God, sacramental celebrations, prayer,
works of penance and charity; (3) gathering, caring for, and building the parish community, communicating with the members, visiting families, helping the sick and the poor, promoting family life;
(4) acquiring and maintaining suitable facilities (church building,
rectory, cemetery) and administering resources, accounts, con-
tracts, and payments (collections, savings, fund drives); (5) mission
outreach and support, spreading the gospel message, promoting
vocations; and (6) promoting social justice, witness and actions on
behalf of the human community.[4] The length of this list emphasizes
the importance of the role of parishioners, and in parishes with only
one priest in residence, these activities would be difficult to carry
out without the participation of the lay members of the parish.

The other key term used often in this book is pastor. Several
canons of the *Code* describe the role and duties of a pastor. He is to
carry out the functions of teaching, sanctifying, and governing with
the cooperation of deacons and assistance of lay members of the
Christian faithful (c. 519). These responsibilities of the pastor are
spelled out more fully in canons 528 and 529. While the canons
explicitly state that only an ordained priest can be the pastor of a
parish (c. 521.1), many of the pastor's functions can be performed by
deacons and laypersons. This is one of the reasons that a nonpriest,

that is, a deacon or layperson, can be placed in charge of a parish when priests are lacking, as canon 517.2 provides.

This new type of leadership by deacons, religious brothers and sisters, married and single laypersons is now a growing phenomenon in Roman Catholic parishes, both nationally and worldwide. Why and how has this come about? The two most important factors facilitating these changes are first, the teachings of the Second Vatican Council that defined the Church as the People of God and stressed the active role and co-responsibility of the laity, based on their baptism and full membership.[5] The second factor is the escalating shortage of priests throughout the world.[6]

Previous Research on Alternate Parish Leadership

Joseph H. Fichter's book, *Wives of Catholic Clergy*, included interviews with wives of Catholic deacons and wives of former Protestant clergy. In 1980 the Holy See gave permission to American bishops to accept married Episcopal clergy into the Catholic priesthood in the United States. Fichter discussed a key restriction by the Catholic Church on the married convert priest's parish work: "To avoid a further possibility of scandal to the faithful, the married priest should be assigned to administrative or educational tasks and kept away from the parochial pastoral ministry."[7]

Fichter found that there were forty-four married convert priests in the United States by 1990. In his words, "This exemplifies the unusual situation where the Catholic Church ordains men who were already married (but does not marry men who are already ordained)."[8]

My own research interest in alternate leadership of parishes was sparked in 1987 when I read a brief announcement in the *National Catholic Reporter* about a bishop who had recently appointed a woman to head a parish in his diocese. That news literally stunned me. As a lifelong Catholic, I could only imagine what a shock it might be for someone to knock on the rectory door and discover that the woman opening the door was not the housekeeper or the secretary, but the pastor! My curiosity was also piqued because of my own research interest in women who were beginning to occupy positions that had previously been reserved for men. These are the factors that led to my earlier research on Catholic women in charge of parishes where there were no resident priests.

That research was carried out during my sabbatical leave in the academic year 1989–90, when I visited twenty Catholic parishes in the four major census regions of the United States, where there were no priests in residence. The people in charge of the twenty parishes were women religious (sisters) and married women. It was my expectation that parishioners who lost their resident priest would be both saddened and angry about that loss because they felt like "second-class citizens" compared to other parishes in the diocese.

An illustration of parishioners' change in attitudes comes from an incident that occurred during that study when I was visiting a small parish in a remote rural area. There a parishioner indicated that there was an additional reason why she wanted her parish to survive. She took me to see the small cemetery adjoining the parish grounds and showed me the plots where her grandparents and great-grandparents were buried. For her, that parish and cemetery constituted sacred ground, and there was no question about her attitude regarding the survival of her parish. She was willing to accept a new form of leadership because she did *not* want her parish to be closed. I found that parishioners like her are willing to dedicate many more hours to working on committees because of the major part the parish plays in their lives.[9]

One of the key findings in my earlier study was that the women leaders (religious sisters as well as married women) practiced collaborative leadership, in contrast to the kind of hierarchical leadership typical of many of the previous pastors in those parishes. Why was this? Did these women tend to opt for non-hierarchical leadership because they were women, or because they were laity?

This question could not be answered with my data on women pastors. Only a similar study of nonpriest male leaders, with equal numbers of clergy and laity, could attempt to answer that question. That is why I embarked on my second study of Catholic parishes, the subject of this book. I am convinced that the more we know about the everyday experiences of the people in these parishes, how they participate in parish activities, and what they think and how they feel about their situation, the better we will understand the implications of what is now a growing phenomenon: Catholic parishes with no resident priests.

My exploratory study of a parish headed by a married man in the summer of 1995 provided a sharper focus for this book[10] During my interview with a group of parishioners whose pastor was a married deacon, a layman who was a long-time member of the parish echoed the sentiments of other male parishioners in that group. He admitted that he and his family had seldom volunteered to participate in parish committee work while their pastors were priests. But he quickly and proudly added that his family is now putting in many more hours of work at the parish because they are keenly aware of his deacon's constraints: a full-time job outside the parish, a working wife, and teenaged children.

What impressed this parishioner most of all, however, was the content of the deacon's sermons. He explained that when the deacon preached, he used examples drawn from his own life with his family at home. "How can I *not* help out?" this parishioner asked. "Our deacon knows what it's like to get up in the middle of the night with a sick child. He's one of us!"

What this parishioner singled out as the most important characteristic of the new parish leader was the deacon's marital status. Prior to my conversation with this parishioner, I had not ruled out the inclusion of parishes headed by religious brothers and other single laymen in my sample of males heading parishes without a resident priest. But his words, "He's one of us," gave me the focus for this study. It was my encounter with that parishioner that convinced me to adopt as a major research concern the impact of *married male leadership* on Roman Catholic parishes.

My current research directly relates to a growing expectation among Catholics that the first group to be designated as a new resource for the priesthood will be married men. How will married priests be received by Roman Catholic parishioners in the United States? Previous research on the attitudes of Catholics in the United States has provided us with some relevant data. For example, a national poll of Catholic laity taken in 1993 by D'Antonio et al. revealed that 72 percent of Catholic laity accept the notion of married men as priests, compared to 52 percent in 1970. A more recent poll taken in 1999 by D'Antonio et al. found that 71 percent still agreed with this change, and they also found that 77 percent agreed that it would be a good thing if priests who have married were returned to active ministry. Also, a national survey of Catholic priests and nuns in 1994 found that the majority of priests (59 percent) and nuns (66 percent) were in favor of allowing priests to marry.[11]

We have information about parishioners' attitudes toward alternate parish leadership from the D'Antonio et al. studies. In the 1993 survey, the following statement was included in the telephone survey:

> If a shortage of priests in the future required a reduction of priestly activities, some changes may occur in parish life. I am going to read a list of six changes which may occur. Please tell me after each if you would be willing to accept it in your home parish. Tell me if it

would be very acceptable, somewhat acceptable, or not
at all acceptable to you.

Some of the parish changes were more acceptable than others.
The majority accepted three of them: "Baptisms performed only by
deacons or lay officials of the church" (63 percent); "no resident
priest in the parish, but only a lay administrator and visiting priests"
(56 percent); and marriages performed by deacons or lay officials"
(51 percent). But fewer than half accepted the remaining three
changes: "less than one Mass a week" (41 percent); "no priest to visit
the sick" (41 percent); and "no priest for the last rites" (30 percent).[12]

In their most recent poll taken in 1999, D'Antonio et al.
eliminated the two questions on baptisms and marriages. The
1999 survey revealed the following: 51 percent accept the lay
administrator (a 5 percentage point decrease from 1993); no
change in percentage accepting less than one Mass a week (41 percent); only 34 percent accept no priest to visit the sick (a 7 percentage point decrease); and only 20 percent accept no priest for
the last rites (a 10 percentage point decrease).[13]

These findings provide a corrective to the limited vision of
those Catholics who, perhaps because they live in an area that
has not yet experienced a serious priest shortage, assume that
deacons or lay administrators would be unacceptable to
Catholics in the United States. While most of the Catholics in
that national study prefer to have at least one Mass per week and
have a priest available to visit the sick and administer the last
rites, over half of them would accept a situation with a lay
administrator and a visiting priest in their parish. These data
may also be helpful to those bishops who, faced with an escalating number of deaths and retirements among their priests, are in
the process of making decisions about appointing nonpriests to
administer parishes.

Necessary Information

What we do not now know is how the leadership of married men in Catholic parishes in the United States is working out in daily situations in the "trenches" of the parish. Surveys have not provided us with such necessary information such as the following: (1) What do these married leaders and the key participants (their wives and children, their parishioners, visiting priests, and bishops) think and feel about this new situation? (2) What are the conditions under which they would find some changes acceptable or not? (3) How do they translate these attitudes into behavior and create new strategies as they interact with each other on a daily basis? (4) What new parish structures are emerging as a result of greater parishioner participation? (5) How do the leaders' key collaborators (parishioners, his family members, priests, and bishops) demonstrate their support or nonsupport of their leadership role? The information that we need in order to have a clearer picture of a growing phenomenon in Catholic parish life cannot be obtained from a survey that gives us a statistical overview, because it fails to provide us with an in-depth view that reveals the thoughts, insights, and strategies of the people involved in this situation.

Because there is a historical precedent for married clergy in the Catholic Church, many scholars predict that allowing married men to be ordained as priests is likely to be the first major change in the present church law regarding church ministry. In the meantime we know that there are already some parishes in our own country where married men are in charge, even though they are not ordained as priests. This book takes us inside twenty of these parishes where parishioners are experiencing alternate forms of leadership for a better understanding of this new form of ministry.

Insights from Sociological Theory

My research on married men as pastors draws on the work of theorists Peter Berger and Thomas Luckmann (1966) to address the aforementioned research questions. Their theory includes three levels of analysis that reveal different aspects about what is going on in their parishes. Like the pictures produced by different camera lenses, the levels of sociological analysis reveal a clearer picture of parish life because each has a different focus.

Berger and Luckmann argue that the production of a new social reality is essentially a *human* production (a process they call *externalization*) whereby individuals, by their own human activity, create their social worlds. This theory views the social order as an ongoing human production and that all social structures are a result of past human activity. As they describe it, "the social order exists only and insofar as human activity continues to produce it." Thus human beings are seen as capable of acting on their own environment, not simply passively accepting whatever the social order dictates.

This theory posits that the strategies used by individuals in everyday life must be taken into account because it is their actions and interactions that bring forth a new social reality. The "individual people" in this study include the following participants in each parish: the new parish leader, members of his parish, his family, the priest who visits the parish on Sundays (the sacramental minister), and the bishop who appointed the married man as the head of the parish.

The second level of analysis focuses on the new structures that are created by individual human beings. Berger and Luckmann's theory states that once the new shared reality created by human beings is given a name, it takes on a life of its own (a process they call *objectivation*). Therefore, an important research goal is to identify the basic structures that have been created in their parishes, like the mode of leadership that was created by the new leader and his congregation, with the cooperation of the visiting priest and the bishop. In this study some of the new structures include: collaborative leadership models, the evolving role of the visiting priest, wives and children's contributions to the parish and to family finances, parishioners participation in parish activities and committees, rectory living for the family members, and supportive structures created by the bishop.

According to Berger and Luckmann, these two processes (externalization and objectivation) occur almost simultaneously. Once a new structure, like a parish council, is not only created, but also named and recognized, it imposes itself on the human beings involved. In other words, once a new reality is objectified, it is visibly "out there" and people may react positively, negatively, ambivalently, or indifferently.

The theory also argues that it is important to ascertain the thoughts and feelings of individual human beings regarding their acceptance of a new social reality, like the parishioners who were highly motivated to volunteer for committee work because their new parish leader shared the joys and sorrows of married life. A case in point is the married parishioner who succinctly explained why all the members of his family were active and committed parishioners with these words: "He's one of us!" At this level of analysis, called internalization, the focus is on the thoughts, motivations, and feelings of individuals involved in the new situation. What Berger and Luckmann argue is that once people interpret a structure as meaningful to them, they will internalize it, and will continue to recreate it by their everyday actions. Their actions, in turn, contribute to the maintenance of the new social reality. On the other hand, those whose feelings and interpretations are negative and fail to internalize the new structure, may remove themselves from the situation or work to change it.

Another research goal, then, is to discover the motivations and feelings of the people involved in the current parish situation: the parishioners, their parish leaders and their families, the visiting priests, and the bishops who appointed these parish leaders. This information will help us to understand why they engage in the actions that continue to recreate and thus to maintain their new parish structures.

Data Collection Procedures

1. Locating the Parishes and the Married Leaders

In order to understand the context of the everyday experiences of parishioners and parish staff in these parishes headed by married men, my first task was to locate the key informants, the married leaders, who, in turn, could help to insure the participation of the other potential interviewees. The chief source was *The Official Catholic Directory 1996*.[14] Searching for the names and addresses of men without the title of "Reverend" who are heading parishes in *The Official Catholic Directory* is like looking for the proverbial needle in the haystack. The publishers of this reference volume must depend on the staff members in chancery offices of the 193 dioceses throughout the United States to supply them with updated information each year, and the thoroughness of the data gathering varies.

Since only the number of parishes, but not their names, are listed in each of these five categories of leadership, one can locate the names of those parishes administered by nonpriests only by a careful reading of all the parishes in each diocese where there was at least one parish administered by a nonpriest. In these cases the name of the person heading the parish appears, usually followed by titles such as pastoral administrator in one diocese or parish director in another. Wherever the title preceding the man's name was either "Rev. Mr." (a deacon's title) or "Deacon" or "Mr." in the case of the laymen, I created another card for my file of potential parishes. Because the title "pastor" is reserved for ordained priests, and no formal title for this new position has been designated thus far, they vary by diocese. In the twenty parishes included in my study, the following titles were given to the married men: "pastoral administrator," "administrator," "parish director," "parochial administrator," "parish life director," and "pastoral coordinator."[15]

It was not difficult to find the name of the parish leader in fifteen of the parishes, because his name alone was listed as the administrator of the parish. But in one of these parishes, he was given the title "Rev." so his leadership as a nonpriest was invisible. In the remaining five parishes, the names of the parish leader were not included in *The Official Catholic Directory*. In these cases only the visiting priest was listed, even though he was residing elsewhere.

In none of these cases was it evident from a reading of the diocesan listings that any of the men heading these parishes had a spouse, and this was my next hurdle. In order to discern their marital status, my strategies included phoning staff persons in the bishop's office, consulting with women pastoral administrators from my previous study, and with colleagues, friends, and church officials. My last resort was to dial the parish phone number and ask the question regarding marital status to whoever answered the telephone.

Another source for information regarding the location of parishes without resident priests can be found in Catholic newspapers and journals that include an employment opportunities section. These ads not only point to parishes where nonpriests may apply for the position, but they also illustrate the kinds of credentials and experience that are required. For this reason I have inserted portions of an advertisement that was published in the employment opportunities section of *National Catholic Reporter* on February 2, 2001.

The Diocese of San Bernardino, Calif. has a job opening for the following position: pastoral coordinator.
Responsibilities include administration, leadership, educational and pastoral care of a parish without a pastor.
Provides for the coordination of religious formation and
education, liturgy and sacramental preparation, community development, social justice and social service
needs. Collaborates with the parish pastoral council and
provides for the formation of volunteer ministers. The
ideal candidate will be a practicing and updated Roman
Catholic with positive, parish-based interpersonal, orga-
nizational and supervisory skills. Must be flexible and a
people motivator. Excellent writing, public speaking and
catechetical skills required. MA degree (or equivalent)
in theology, religious studies, pastoral studies, religious
education or related field is preferred. Candidates must
be sensitive to a multi-cultural, Southern California
environment. Some assigned positions may require
bilingual (English/Spanish) skills.

2. Locations within the Census Regions

My objective was to have a sample of twenty parishes
headed by married men, with equal numbers of parishes in the
four major census regions. This proved to be an unachievable
goal. Although it was possible to locate at least five of these
parishes in the Midwest, South, and Western regions, my intensive efforts to locate five of them in the Eastern census region
were unsuccessful. My telephone calls to diocesan offices located
in this region failed to uncover any additional parishes for my
study. Over and over again, I was told by priests, bishops, and
other diocesan staff persons located in the Eastern region of the
country that they were unaware of any parishes that were administered by married men.

The historical study of the Roman Catholic parishes in the United States between 1850 and 1980 edited by Jay Dolan[16] sheds some light on my dilemma. Dolan explains that parish life in different parts of the country developed in different ways, depending on the ethnic background of the parishioners. The parishes in the Northeastern part of the country where Catholics first settled, for example, tend to have more priests assigned per parish, more "national" (ethnically identified) parishes, and more established patterns of clerical leadership than do those in other regions of the country. By contrast, the parishes in the Southeastern and South Central part of the country are characterized by fewer Catholics and a dearth of resources and personnel. Dolan summarizes by stating, "Of all the regions in the United States, the Midwest was the most significant in terms of nurturing the reforms of Vatican II."[17]

It is no wonder then, that by the spring of 1996 I was able to locate only one parish headed by a married man in the entire Eastern census region. As the supply of priests begins to dry up, some bishops, rather than appointing a nonpriest to administer a parish, have resorted to actions such as closing and/or combining parishes, reducing the number of priests in diocesan offices and teaching positions, recruiting priests from other countries, encouraging priests seventy years and older to continue as pastors, and increasing the number of parishes administered by neighboring priest pastors. My final list of twenty parishes consisted of seven parishes situated in the Midwest, six each in the South and the West, and one in the Northeast.

Although I had planned to include an equal number of rural and urban parishes in my previous study of parishes entrusted to women, only two of the parishes in the entire country with that type of leadership at that time (1989) could be described as urban or suburban, thus only two of the twenty parishes in my earlier study were located in urban areas.

On the other hand, when I began to comb *The Official Catholic Directory* in the spring of 1996 I found that the description of "alternate parish leadership" as an almost exclusively rural phenomenon was beginning to change with the continuing escalation of the priest shortage. By 1996 the following dioceses had nonpriests heading urban and suburban parishes: Austin, Baltimore, Baton Rouge, Chicago, Cincinnati, Colorado Springs, Corpus Christi, Fort Worth, Fresno, Indianapolis, Knoxville, Louisville, Memphis, Milwaukee, Phoenix, Richmond, Saginaw, Spokane, and Toledo. Because of these changes, I was able to find an equal number of urban and rural parishes for this study.

3. Contacting the Parish Leaders and Bishops

After I selected the twenty parishes administered by married men, the task of persuading them to participate in this research project loomed before me. My strategy was to write a letter of invitation to the parish leader, followed up by a telephone call about a week after the letter arrived. The letter contained the following information: my credentials (professor of sociology, specializing in the sociology of religion) and my interest in the new forms of ministry in parishes throughout the United States. Other credentials that were meant to be "persuaders" were the following: my Catholic background and my age (63), my earlier study of women pastors, and the names and phone numbers of three references (two priests and one religious sister) who are well-known as experts on parish life. I learned later that these references sometimes functioned as "door openers" for me in the parishes.

In my letter to the parish leader I also explained my proposed schedule: to arrive at the parish on a Friday and leave on a Monday; participate in all of the weekend liturgies and other parish activities; and interview him, his wife, a group of parishioners, the priest serving as the sacramental minister, and the bishop. I informed him that that my visit would not be a financial burden on the parish, thanks to my research grant. During the follow-up phone call I invited him to ask any other questions he had regarding this project.

The letter and phone call were successful. Only one of the men declined my invitation to participate in the study because he and his wife were already in the midst of packing to leave the parish and move to another location for their retirement. Three others were not participants because I discovered during the phone call that their church was officially designated not as a parish, but as a mission.

My next task was to persuade the local bishop to agree to an interview while I was in his diocese. I usually telephoned his secretary to discern when he had free time on his schedule during my stay in his diocese. My follow-up letter, asking him to participate, was similar to the letter sent to the parish leader. I then telephoned the bishops directly and all of them agreed to participate. One of the bishops was due to undergo major surgery, and we were not able to schedule an interview during my visit to his diocese. By the end of May 1996, I completed the scheduling of the twenty parish visits and was ready to move to the next phase of the research process: my visits to these parishes.

4. Traveling to Research Sites and Gaining Access to Information

Armed with my tape recorder and interview schedules, I began my travels to the twenty research sites in early June 1996 and finished the data gathering in late February 1997. This period was an unforgettable journey into towns, villages, and cities that were unfamiliar to me. Once I arrived at the airport and rented a car, I paid close attention to the detailed directions to the church that the parish leader had sent me.

A trip that stands out in my memory was one that required flights on four airplanes to reach my destination. The last flight, taken after an overnight stay, was in a four-seater plane that landed on an airstrip in a remote Native American village. Here I needed no maps because there were no paved roads. The only vehicles were small open cars with oversized tires. With the exception of a few raised plank sidewalks situated in the central parts of the village, most walking was on dirt paths. The buildings in this small village of approximately five hundred Native Americans consisted almost entirely of small homes, a school, and two small grocery stores. I learned that all but a handful of people in this village were Catholic, which explains why two of the four largest buildings were a Catholic church and a parish office building with housing for the two priests who ministered to five other villages in addition to this one. Because there were no motels and the assisting priests were away on a retreat during my visit, they arranged for me to stay at the parish house.

Knowing these living arrangements in advance, the young man who directed me to the parish house smilingly asked, "Are you a church representative?" "No," I replied. But I quickly added that I worked at a university, and that my research was about church leadership. This seemed to satisfy him. I learned later that the visiting priest had assured the parishioners in this village that I was not a government employee. The bishop subsequently informed me that the native people in his diocese were both tired and wary of government-sponsored research, so my reply to this young man was very important. Though I was an outsider, my university affiliation and our shared affiliation with the Catholic Church had helped to reassure the young parishioner.

Throughout my journeys to these parishes I was conscious of the fact that I was a stranger intruding in the lives of my subjects and dependent on them to make a sacrifice of their time in order to provide me with the information I needed. I am extremely grateful to them for their cooperation, a crucial element in this type of research. Many of them told me that they had never met a sociologist before. Not only was I a stranger by profession, but also I had never lived in any of these cities or towns. Most of the parishioners had been told that my home was in Washington, D.C. As I mentioned, my place of residence could have been a major problem in the Native American village, where a "Washington, D.C. visitor" meant "federal agent" to the people living there. In this case, therefore, my nongovernmental affiliation was advantageous.

Once I arrived at each parish and had access to the interviewees, I was then faced with the problem of access to information. In each parish the length of my visit was usually four days. Because I had very little time to get acquainted with them prior to the interviews, I developed some strategies that I hoped would succeed in making people comfortable enough to share their experiences, their strategies, and their thoughts and feelings with me.

First of all, I began my visit by taking the family of the parish leader to dinner at a nearby restaurant as a way of "breaking the ice," getting acquainted, and thanking them in advance for the time they would be devoting to this project. This typically took place on the first evening of the day I arrived and before I conducted any formal interviews. During this meal I learned the names of family members, and they had a chance to ask any questions they had about the study and about their role in it. We learned a lot about each other during that dinner, and I am convinced that it facilitated the whole research experience.

For two reasons the parish in the Native American village was the only one where this family dinner did not take place: the lack of a restaurant and the pastoral administrator's time constraints with his dual role as parish leader and tribal chief. During my stay there, he was away much of the time, helping at churches in two other Native American villages while the priests were gone, and presiding at the burial of a relative at another village.

There were, on the other hand, similar "getting acquainted" events that took place in the village. On two occasions parish families invited me to share a meal with them. Also, I invited a female elder who had "adopted me" to have lunch with me at the parish house. From the day of my arrival she had taken me under her wing, introduced me to her family and other parishioners, showed me where the stores were located, and accompanied me to the tribal dance.

5. Conducting the Interviews

During the four days in each parish, from Friday through Monday, I conducted taped individual interviews with the married man heading the parish, his wife, the visiting priest who celebrated Sunday Mass in the parish, and the bishop who appointed the married man to lead the parish. These were face-to-face interviews, with the exception of two of the bishops and two of the priests, who were interviewed by telephone.

In each parish I taped a focus group interview with parishioners who represented the gender, age, racial, and ethnic groups of the parish. These group interviews, ranging from four to twenty persons, with an average of eight in each group, typically lasted from forty-five minutes to an hour. All of these group interviews were held in the parish hall or in a parish office, with the exception of three parishes where the interviews were held in the dining room of the parish house because there was no parish hall. I also conducted group interviews with the children of the pastor. All of these, with the exception of one daughter away at college, were held in their homes. I asked the same open-ended questions on all of the interviews in each parish.

The consent form required for the interviewing of human subjects that was read and signed by each interviewee before the audiotaping began also helped to elicit their cooperation. The form clearly explained that each person's name would be kept strictly confidential, and that no identifying information, like the name of the diocese, city, or parish would be used in any written or oral report of the study. During some of my sessions with the parishioner groups, I could almost sense a sigh of relief in the room as they read the consent form. While I was answering questions before they signed the form, some of the interviewees sent verbal and nonverbal cues that they would cooperate and share their insights with me. On the other hand, there were some parishioners who were disappointed when they learned that their names would not appear in my book. Some of them complained that this meant they were losing a chance to go down in history! When I replied that I would lose my job if I revealed their names, they good-naturedly cooperated.

The goal of my research, a better understanding of what was going on in these parishes without resident priests, was appealing to my interviewees. They had survived not only the shock on hearing that they were to have a new type of parish leader, but they had also gone through a grieving process following the loss of their priest pastor. Like the women pastors in my earlier study, they were making their way through a minefield of mistakes, rejections, and hurt feelings and then getting on with the business of keeping their parish open and operating. Their typical reaction was that they wanted to share their experiences with others who would be faced with the same situation in the future.

Although I had taken a course on focus group interviews, this was the first research project where I conducted group interviews. It was also the first time I had ever interviewed bishops or children, and I was especially apprehensive about establishing rapport with them. Even though my visit to their parish was short, I wanted to find as many ways as possible to convince all of my interviewees to share their experiences, thoughts, and feelings about the parish situation with me. Therefore, before I turned on the tape recorder, I made a point of explaining how and why sociologists like me put so much time and effort into research projects like this one. I knew the "why" part could be a key factor for eliciting their support, so I presented two ways of explaining why sociologists do research. The first one that I learned while I was in graduate school was to "contribute to the accumulation of knowledge in the discipline." Their typical response was a polite smile or a nodding of the head.

It was the second rationale, however, that elicited a very strong response. I quoted the late sociologist Father Joseph Fitzpatrick, S.J., a professor at Fordham University, widely recognized for his pioneering research on Puerto Rican immigrants in the United States. I had heard him articulate his own motivation for research at an annual meeting of the Society for the Scientific Study of Religion in 1994, two years before his death. During a session in which he was honored for his life-long research, someone in the audience asked him why he was still engaged in doing research. Father Fitzpatrick replied, "Well, I know I'm eighty-four years old, and I did retire from teaching when I turned seventy. But as long as I can, I want to continue to contribute to the unfolding of the mysteries of God's creation."

I'll always be thankful that I was there to hear his reply and that I recorded his words in my notebook, because his rationale resonated with my own beliefs about the importance of research. Since my interviewees were practicing Catholics, it should be no surprise that there was a strong positive reaction when they heard the words "to contribute to the unfolding of the mysteries of God's creation." Their typical response was, "What would you like to know?" My best example of this reaction occurred during my first interview with a bishop. Prior to this interview, a friend who had spent some time working in a diocesan office, advised me to keep the bishops' interviews short because of their busy schedules. The strategy she suggested was to "stand up after twenty minutes and make preparations to leave." In this case, however, the bishop, who had fully cooperated as soon as he heard Father

Fitzpatrick's quote, insisted that I remain seated because he wanted to complete the interview. Then toward the end of our session, when I reminded the bishop that it was time for my departure to the airport, he insisted on walking me to my car so that he could continue talking!

Other interviewees who presented a challenge to me at the beginning of this project were the children of the parish leader. Like the bishops, they represented another group that I had not previously interviewed. My usual strategy was to wait until the end of my visit to their home before I interviewed the children. By that time they had met me during our dinner in a restaurant, had seen me both in church when their father introduced me to the congregation, and also when I came to their home to interview their mother. Nonetheless, on the day before I was leaving, during dinner at the living quarters in the rectory (where that family lived), I sensed that the three children might still be apprehensive about the upcoming interview session, and spoke to their mother about it. Following her suggestion, I invited them to go out with me for ice cream. By the time we returned home, the children not only agreed to the interview, but they wanted to be assured that I use the tape recorder with them, just as I had with their parents. Soon after we started the tape, the youngest child asked if I would rewind the tape so she could hear what she sounded like. On hearing her voice, she clapped her hands, and was an enthusiastic interviewee from that moment on.

The Native American village was a place where I faced a possible language problem conducting the group interview with parishioners. Two of the Native American "elders" who were participating in the interview spoke only their native language, so I hired one of the women in the village to serve as a translator. I was deeply impressed with the patience and deference of the younger Native Americans toward their elders in that interview session. Each time I asked a question, they made sure that it was translated so that the elders could reply before I moved on to the next question. This turned out to be the longest group interview in my study, almost four hours in all, but no one complained. Likewise, without translators at all three of the Mexican-American parishes, access to important information from the older parishioners, and from some of the others who were not fluent in English, would have been missing.

Another strategy that I used for access to information was to bring a copy of my book on women pastors with me so that the parish leader could peruse it while I was in his parish. Although most of these leaders had heard of it, only a handful had read it in its entirety. It turned out to be particularly helpful on my last two site visits when I decided to send a copy of the book to the parish leaders prior to my arrival. Because they had enough time to read the book before I arrived, these men had a clearer idea of the research process itself. They also had a sense of how the experiences of people in their parishes might be helpful to parishioners and future parish leaders like themselves throughout the country. This not only gave me easier access to the information, but it also saved a lot of time explaining the various logistics of this project.

In fact, on my arrival at the last site, the parish leader, who had read the entire book, operated somewhat like a member of my research team, alerting me to upcoming committee meetings and other parish gatherings that I might attend in order to acquaint myself with the parish and the parishioners. He kept thinking of ways that I could obtain more data, and he was very thoughtful about choosing a representative group of parishioners for the focus group. He also told me that reading the book convinced him that I had kept my promise of anonymity to the women pastors. As in other parishes I visited, he had written an announcement in the weekly parish bulletin informing the entire parish about my impending arrival and the goals of my research. The section of the bulletin called "From the Parish Director" included the following information:

> We are pleased to welcome Dr. Ruth Wallace from George Washington University, Washington, D.C. (Sorry if some of you were expecting the other Dr. Ruth!) Dr. Wallace is a sociologist who conducted a national study on parish directors. At that time, the vast majority of parish directors were women, and only rural parishes had parish directors. Dr. Wallace, with a grant from the Lilly Foundation, is now completing a study of men parish directors. Dr. Wallace will be looking into and observing our interactions this weekend. We welcome Dr. Wallace into our midst and we are honored to be part of this national study.

When this parish leader introduced me during Mass on Sunday, he asked me to stand and raise my hand so the parishioners would recognize me (as other pastors had done), and he encouraged the parishioners to speak with me afterward. The fact that he was so cooperative and was looking for chances to make my visit more fruitful I would attribute, at least in part, to his greater awareness and understanding of my research on women pastors.

Most of my interviews with the parish leaders, lasting from one to two hours, took place in the parish office. Completing the interview with one of the parish leaders required several sessions of shorter length because this man was not only the parish leader, but he also had a full-time job outside the parish. The group interview with parishioners was usually scheduled after the last Mass on Sunday in the church basement or parish office. The wives and children were typically interviewed in their family home, and in five cases their home was the parish rectory. It was necessary to schedule two separate interview sessions for three of the wives with full-time jobs outside the parish in order to complete the interview schedule. Two of these interviews were conducted while the wife and I took a long walk in a park, and one of the children was interviewed while we ate lunch at a restaurant near her college campus.

Nine of the sacramental ministers were interviewed after the last Mass on Sunday. Of these, seven took place in the parish rectory and two in the church itself. Three of the four priests who were traveling from long distances to help out in two or more parishes were interviewed after Mass during lunch at a local restaurant. One priest was unable to schedule a face-to-face interview, so I interviewed him by telephone while I was in his diocese. Another priest who was on a tight schedule met me in a downtown park where I conducted the interview. Six of the priests were scheduled for an interview in their own rectories in a neighboring parish. When I arrived at the rectory of one of them, I discovered that he had been called to the hospital to administer to a dying parishioner. This occurred on the morning I was booked for a departure flight, so I left a message at his rectory, and scheduled a telephone interview with him later.

All of the bishops had agreed to schedule an interview and, with three exceptions, I visited their offices to interview them. I interviewed one of the bishops while eating lunch in a local restaurant, the only time available on his schedule. Another bishop, because of a conflict in schedules, agreed to be interviewed by telephone after my visit to his diocese. One bishop, who was taken to the hospital shortly before I arrived in his diocese, never recovered from what turned out to be a terminal illness. All of the bishops were cooperative during the interview. In fact, three of them, at the conclusion of our session, encouraged me to speak with one of their staff members who served as a direct contact for the pastoral administrators in the diocese. These conversations also provided helpful information. In all, I completed 111 interviews with key informants: 20 with the married parish leaders, 20 with their wives, 12 with their children,[18] 20 with their parishioners, 20 with their visiting priests, and 19 with their bishops.

6. Other Data Resources

At the research sites, I also made observations while I was participating in the parish activities that took place during my visit. These included Sunday Masses, weekday word and communion services, coffee and doughnut gatherings after Mass, and parish committee meetings. I spoke informally with parishioners before and after these occasions, and with some of the office staff members while we shared a meal during lunch breaks.

One of the parish leaders invited me to accompany him on his visit to the home of an elderly parishioner who was bedridden. While there, I participated in the communion service, and had a short conversation with the parishioner before we left. In another parish a lay leader and his wife encouraged me to accompany them on a visit to a very poor parishioner living in an isolated rural area. In situations like these, I was able to observe how the men interacted with their parishioners, and added this information to my field notes that I recorded on tape during my visit. Additional information was gleaned from parish bulletins and other written materials gathered while I was at each research site.

When I returned from each research site, my research assistant began the process of transcribing the interview tapes. Once the transcriptions were finished, I coded them, and using these codes, my research assistant retrieved the data, using HyperResearch™ software. I then analyzed the data and began the final stage of my research: the writing process.

This book is a journey to the twenty parishes where people shared their experiences, perceptions, and feelings so that we might better understand their unique situation. The following six chapters present my research findings on the key participants: the deacon and lay pastoral administrators (chapter 2), their wives (chapter 3), their children (chapter 4), the parishioners (chapter 5), the priests (chapter 6), and the bishops (chapter 7). The concluding chapter summarizes the research findings, suggests some implications for future research and for policy changes, and concludes with a glimpse of a different form of leadership for Roman Catholic parishes. It is my hope that the information in this book will "contribute to the unfolding of the mysteries of God's creation."

Chapter 2

Parish Leadership: Deacon and Lay Comparisons

One of the most important findings in my earlier study of Catholic parishes headed by women was that all the women practiced collaborative leadership, in contrast to the hierarchical style of many of the previous priest pastors. This chapter spotlights the leadership styles of the married male leaders and compares the leadership styles of deacons with those of laymen, beginning with a profile of the twenty married men. The rest of the chapter presents findings about parish leaders with respect to clerical status, marital status, race and gender issues, and collaborative leadership.

Characteristics of the Twenty Married Men

When I interviewed them in 1996–97, the average age of the married men was fifty-one, ranging from the youngest who was thirty-eight years old to the oldest who was sixty-eight.[1] Only one was in his thirties, nine were in their forties, seven in their fifties, and three in their sixties. Froehle and Gautier report that the average age of diocesan priests in active ministry in the United States in 2000 was fifty-nine, somewhat older than the men in my study.[2] With respect to the duration of the twenty marriages, the range was from five to forty-one years, and the average was twenty-four years.

These men were not lacking appropriate experience for this particular occupation. Keep in mind that most Catholic bishops in the United States did not appoint nonpriests to head parishes until after 1983, and the vast majority of those early appointments were women religious with master's degrees in theology.[3] The married male leaders in this study averaged four years on their present job as pastoral administrators. Two of the men I visited were in their first year as the head of a parish, four had completed two years, six had completed three or four years, four had completed five or six years, and the four most experienced had completed from seven to nine years.

Neither their educational backgrounds nor their former jobs were totally unrelated to their present work. Five of them had spent from one to seven years in the seminary in preparation for the priesthood. The laymen were more highly educated than the deacons. All ten of them had college degrees (eight master's, one doctorate, and one bachelor's degree). By contrast only four of the deacons had college degrees (three bachelor's and one master's), and of the remaining six deacons, three had some college and the three with high school diplomas only were stationed in poor parishes in remote parts of the country. Although all of the deacons completed the diaconate program before ordination, this program does not award a degree, but is similar to other certificate programs in that it typically consists of weekend courses over a three- or four-year period.

Most of the educational specializations of the twenty pastoral administrators were relevant to their present work in the parish. Five of them majored in theology or religious studies, five in education, three in pastoral studies or counseling, and one each in agriculture, pharmacy, and anthropology. The remaining four were deacons who mentioned the diaconate program as their specialization. All viewed much of their prior work experience as a good preparation for their present job. Their former jobs could be classified in three areas: church related, education and counseling, and community or business related. The job categories are listed here.

1. Church-related work: All ten deacons mentioned earlier pastoral work as a deacon, though this work is usually voluntary, not salaried. Of the prior church-related jobs, the position listed by

seven of the men was parish director of religious education. The following jobs were mentioned twice: director of diocesan programs, pastoral assistant, RCIA (Rite of Christian Initiation of Adults), youth ministry, and religious education. Other church-related jobs mentioned once were choir director, pastoral counselor, director of pastoral center, hospital chaplain, hospital pastoral director, parish liturgy leader, parish social outreach programs, and family ministry.

2. Education and counseling: Seven had been high school teachers, two were high school principals, and one was a psychotherapist.

3. Community or business: Ten of the men listed administrative or managerial positions, including local community organization, social service administration, nursing home administration, laboratory supervisor, director of public information, customer relations, Boy Scout district executive, and restaurant manager. Three others listed the following work that also has relevance to their work as pastor: musician, writer, and home improvement contractor. The latter may not seem related to parish work at first glance, but this parish leader was assigned to a poor parish with buildings constantly in need of repair. Building maintenance was, for many of these men, not a small concern.

Thirteen (seven laymen and six deacons) were working in the parish on a full-time basis when I interviewed them. Full-time salaries ranged from $15,000, to $40,000 per year. A deacon in a very poor parish had the lowest salary. The average (mean) salary was $31,685.

Of the seven part-timers, four were deacons and three were laymen. There is an expectation that deacons will engage in full-time paid work outside the parish. Therefore, much of their parish work is voluntary, and this sets them off from the laymen. For instance, one of the deacons, who had a full-time job outside the parish, also worked fifteen hours a week as the pastoral administrator. In addition to his paid work, he also devoted ten hours per week to volunteer ministry work, because it was a requirement for the deacons in his diocese.

It is not surprising, then, that four of the six men whose pastoral work was part time were deacons. Their salaried work included: full-time high school teaching, full-time laboratory supervision, part-time management for the tribal council, and part-time brokering in a printing business. One of the laymen received a part-time salary for his parish work, but he in fact worked full time as the parish leader. Although he had no other paying job, his wife's full-time job allowed him to pursue the work he felt called to do. Another layman was paid part-time for his work as parish leader, but his two other diocesan jobs added up to a full salary.

Only after the visits to all the research sites were completed did I have a complete picture of the characteristics of the twenty parishes and their married leaders that is seen in Table 1.

We can see in the table showing the characteristics of parishes and leaders that ten of the parishes are located in rural areas and ten in urban/suburban areas. Five of the ten rural parishes are located in the Midwest, two in the South, two in the West, and one in the Northeast. Of the ten urban/suburban parishes, four each are located in the West and South, and two are located in the Midwest.

Ten of the parish leaders were deacons and ten were laymen. Regionally, seven parishes were in the Midwest, six each in the South and West, and one in the Northeast. With regard to the racial/ethnic dimension in the parishes, 70 percent (14) were white, 15 percent (3) Hispanic, 10 percent (2) African American, and 5 percent (1) Native American. The racial/ethnic profile of the parish leaders—75 percent (15) white, 15 percent (3) Hispanic, 5 percent (1) African American, and 5 percent (1) Native American—matches the parish profile with one exception: an urban parish in the South in a predominantly African American parish that is headed by a white deacon. The ramifications of this situation are mentioned later in this chapter.[4]

TABLE 1

Characteristics of Parishes and Leaders

		Parishes		Parish Leaders	
	Rural/Urban	Census Region*	Race/Ethnicity	Race/Ethnicity	Deacon/Lay
1	Rural	Midwest	White	White	Lay
2	Rural	Midwest	White	White	Lay
3	Rural	Northeast	White	White	Deacon
4	Rural	West	Native American	Native American	Deacon
5	Rural	West	White	White	Lay
6	Rural	South	White	White	Lay
7	Rural	Midwest	White	White	Deacon
8	Rural	Midwest	White	White	Deacon
9	Rural	South	White	White	Lay
10	Rural	Midwest	White	White	Lay
11	Urban	South	Hispanic	Hispanic	Deacon
12	Suburban	West	White	White	Lay
13	Urban	South	African American	African American	Deacon
14	Urban	West	Hispanic	Hispanic	Deacon
15	Urban	South	African American	White	Deacon
16	Urban	Midwest	White	White	Deacon
17	Urban	West	Hispanic	Hispanic	Deacon
18	Suburban	West	White	White	Lay
19	Urban	South	White	White	Lay
20	Urban	Midwest	White	White	Lay

*Northeast (Middle Atlantic and New England); Midwest (East and West North Central); South (Southeast and Southwest); West (Rocky Mountain and Pacific).

Focusing on their status in the Catholic Church, we see that the deacons are equally distributed in the Midwest, West, and South (three in each of these census regions), and the only parish leader located in the Northeast is also a deacon. The ten laymen are also equally distributed in the West and South (three in each), but four of the lay leaders are located in the Midwest. The deacons and lay leaders are almost equally distributed in urban/suburban and rural parishes. The parishes of six of the deacons are in urban/suburban areas and four are in rural areas, whereas the parishes of six of the laymen are located in rural areas and four in urban/suburban areas.

All eight of the urban/suburban churches were situated in lower class areas in the inner city or at the edge of town. The parishioners in three of these were predominantly Mexican American, three white, and two African American. The parishioners in two of the three white urban parishes were located in neighborhoods that were predominantly African American.

On the other hand, the two suburban parishes were predominantly white and middle class. One of the churches was situated on a college campus, where many worshipers on Sunday were college students. While I was visiting in the other suburban parish, the parishioners were temporarily meeting in a public school auditorium for their Sunday services, because the parish had only recently been established. But they were in the planning stage of providing a building and offices for their church, and proudly showed me the location of the future church buildings, situated on the top of a hill with a wonderful view of the valley below. Parishioners in another small urban parish were attending Sunday Mass in a former Protestant church.

Nine of the ten rural parishes were small, white, and poor. The parishioners themselves built the small wooden church in the Native American village. The parishioners in one of the poor rural areas were meeting in a rented "storefront" church when I visited their site. The only middle-class parish was situated in a rural area that attracted many vacationers in the summer months. The parishioners were also in the midst of building an expansion for their church while I was visiting them.

Deacons: Constraints and Opportunities

Picture yourself sitting in a Roman Catholic church during a Sunday Mass. The priest enters from the back of the church, clad in a long white garment with a flowing green outer vestment and a matching green band around his neck. But you also notice that the priest is preceded by two altar servers and another man. This man, who walks directly in front of the priest, is wearing the same kind of long white garment and green band. However he is not wearing a green outer vestment, and his green band is worn over his left shoulder to denote that he is a deacon.

To your surprise, you observe that when they reach the altar, it is the deacon, not the priest, who steps to the microphone to greet the parishioners and introduce newcomers in the congregation. He then joins the priest at the altar, and during Mass, he leads one of the major prayers, the Kyrie Eleison (Lord have mercy). A little later, after a parishioner reads the epistle, the deacon kneels before the priest to receive his blessing, and proceeds to the podium where he reads the Gospel and delivers a homily.

Later, during the Offertory, the deacon also announces the petitions, and shortly after the consecration, the most solemn part of the Mass, he holds the chalice while the priest holds the small gold dish containing the host. Together they present the body and blood of Christ to the congregation. Just before the communion, at the moment for the kiss of peace he walks out into the congregation with the priest to greet the parishioners, and later assists the priest in distributing communion. Toward the end of Mass, it is the deacon who announces to the congregation that the Mass is over, and then the priest gives his blessing to the people.

To many Catholic laity, this scene would resemble a concelebrated Mass, a Mass that is celebrated together by two priests or more. Confusing? Yes. Unthinkable? No. As in half of the parishes I visited, this one was headed by a married man who was an ordained deacon.

The Greek word, *diakonia*, means service. The role of deacon evolved from a focus on works of charity in the early church to the final step for a seminarian prior to his priestly ordination. However, during the deliberations of Vatican II, the diaconate was restored as a separate ministry of service, and as of 1967, it was again open to married men as well as celibates. Although the main ministries for permanent deacons continue to be charitable works and administration, the ministry of the word and liturgy are also included. Froehle and Gautier describe the deacon's liturgical roles:

> This is defined as performing baptisms, distributing the Eucharist, witnessing and blessing marriages, and bringing viaticum to the dying, as well as officiating at funerals and burial services. Deacons also preside at worship and prayer, and have roles at Mass, including reading the Gospel and preaching.[5]

Looking through a photograph album that depicted a deacon's activities in one of the parishes enabled me to grasp the extent of his duties and privileges as a member of a higher status group in the church, and to contrast his participation with that of a lay pastor. Early pictures showed the deacon in his alb[6] and stole standing next to the bishop on his ordination day, strong reminders of his clerical office. A number of pictures showed him in the act of baptizing children, whereas a layman would need special permission to baptize, except in the case of imminent death. Only in a few extremely isolated regions in the United States, like Alaska, where the priest shortage is acute, are lay pastoral administrators baptizing their parishioners on a regular basis. Several pictures showed the deacon presiding at marriages, an activity which a layman could almost never engage in, unless his bishop received special permission from Rome.

Although the sacrament of the anointing of the sick is not a deacon's prerogative, he can administer viaticum (Eucharist given to a person in danger of death). Deacons can also officiate at funeral ceremonies held outside of the Mass. One of the Hispanic deacons, who headed a large and predominantly Hispanic urban parish, said that he not only "did a lot of funerals," but also presided at all of the baptisms for Spanish-speaking families, fifteen of them in the past month. And, he added,

> I do all the witnessing of marriages here. Here in this community they have gotten used to not having a wedding in the context of a Mass. We do it in a celebration of a communion service.

The deacons, by virtue of their ordination, are members of the clergy, and therefore are placed in a more privileged position, or "higher class," in the church than laymen. Since the status of permanent deacons was reintroduced after Vatican II, some people are often unsure of the privileges and responsibilities attached to that role. A bishop who pointed to a positive aspect of choosing a deacon as a parish leader, also provided an example of another bishop's misunderstanding of a deacon's position in the church when he said,

> One of the advantages of the ordained ministry, particularly with married deacons and their families, it's kind of what I call a theological bridge between the ordained ministry and the baptized ministry. But that person *is* *ordained*, and we have to remember that. Another bishop said to me, just after he ordained his first deacon, "Oh, isn't it wonderful now we have our lay deacon?" And I said, "Once the man is ordained a deacon, he's no longer a layman."

What this bishop was pointing out was that the term "lay deacon" is an oxymoron. Although the deacons are ordained, and have joined the ranks of the clergy, they are not on a par with others in that category. Ordination in the Roman Catholic Church represents a continuum, ranging from deacons (the lowest ranking) to priests, and finally to bishops (a category that includes archbishops, cardinals, and popes). So in a sense the deacons could best be described as on the first rung of a clerical ladder with several steps.

One of the bishops in my study explained the conditions under which deacons could wear a Roman collar. He said that basically only those deacons who work as chaplains in prisons or in hospitals are allowed to wear it so that they would be identified as clergy. He added, "Part of that is for protection and security, especially in the prisons."

Another bishop said that there was some misunderstanding about the term of office for a deacon, and he called it "an evolving role that is not totally understood." He recalled an incident that occurred when he was a pastor in a parish with two deacons:

> One of the very faithful, very involved Catholics, an older man came up to me and said, "How much longer is so and so going to be a deacon? When does his term run out?" He was just amazed when I told him that he was ordained for life as a deacon. And the man just did not understand that. Now the people accepted the ministries of these deacons extremely well, but they were seen as the volunteer who was elevated to some special recognition.

Some Catholics argue that the age factor makes a difference in the acceptance of deacons. For instance, an assisting priest argued that older parishioners would prefer having a deacon as their pastoral administrator. He said,

> I found that the older parishioners were more willing to accept communion, or listen to somebody in the pulpit if they were a deacon, or if they were a sister. But when a layperson gets up there, they feel much freer to disagree with them....We really have to ask, "Who should be in

the pulpit?" What does it take to be in the pulpit? The laity I know can certainly match most of the clergy that I know. It isn't just theology. I think you have to take time to pray over what you're doing. You can't depend on your homily notes, no matter how good they are.

A bishop carefully explained that some ordained deacons have the authority to preach and some do not. He emphasized that some deacons limit their ministries to nonliturgical areas, such as visiting the sick and homebound or running the food pantry, and they have neither the desire nor the training to preach.

Another element that sets the deacons apart from both the priests and the lay pastoral administrators in my study is the educational preparation for this position. One of the bishops who visited other dioceses with permanent diaconate programs described the training as "very poor." He said that it was "more like a lay ministry formation program." A lay pastor with a master's degree explained that the deacons' training in his diocese consisted of two Saturdays a month for four or five years, and he described it as "not academically the same kind of training that I have experienced."

A deacon expressed the need for more training prior to heading a parish:

They left me to flounder by myself with very little direction, guidance, help. I mean I could call the chancery, which I did many a time to find out, "What do I do with this?" Or I did have other priest friends that I would contact and say, "What do I do? How do I do this?" We had tribunal training, annulments and all that, but it's a little different when you're out in the trenches and working.

As the employment advertisement in the previous chapter illustrated, dioceses in the United States that have recruited

pastoral administrators have educational and experiential requirements for the position of pastoral administrator, but they are not
uniform throughout the country. Typically, the requirements are
either a master's degree in theology, pastoral ministry, religious
education, or another field related to parish ministry, or a bachelor's degree in any of these fields, plus six years of parish experience. Some of them stipulate that the candidates must have
worked successfully in a church-related ministry in the diocese for
at least six years, and are familiar with the policies and procedures
governing parish ministry in the diocese.

Another aspect of a deacon's training, which also sets him
apart from a layman, is that the wives of deacons are encouraged
to attend the formation classes with their husbands. Several
women described how they made the long drive to the classes with
their husbands every other week, in good and bad weather.
However, they did not complain, because they saw it as an opportunity to understand more clearly what their husband's new role
would entail. By the end of this training period, all of these wives
have virtually completed the formal study required of their deacon husbands. They also realize that they cannot be ordained as
deacons because they are women.

One of the wives, whose husband had been ordained a deacon seven years prior to his appointment as head of a parish,
pointed out that the training sessions she and her husband
attended in those days did not include any specific preparation for
parish administration.

A visiting priest used the term "mini-priest" when he criti-
cized the deacons' training program in his diocese. He argued that
it engendered the notion that deacons were "mini-priests." This
came up several times, especially in interviews with priests and
bishops. One of the bishops who had described himself as one
who had quite a bit of experience with the diaconal community,

described the deacon's role as "a connector between the market-place and the church:

> My basic sense would be that we don't see a deacon's role primarily as being a mini-priest. He's a sign of service to the community, a connector between the marketplace and the church. I don't think that just because a person happens to be a deacon should he necessarily be an administrator. I think it deals more with the quality of his skills in terms of overseeing, rather than his being a deacon.

Another characteristic that was helpful for eight of these new parish leaders was their status as parish "insiders." As parishioners they had a "stake" in the parish, since they had already invested time, energy, and money in their church community. When I interviewed parishioners in this type of situation, they agreed that it would have been more difficult to accept the married man as the parish leader if they had not known him previously. In fact, one of these parishioners used the term "stabilizing factor" when discussing his acceptance of their new leader.

Six of the deacons were serving as parish leaders in their own parishes, whereas only three of the lay leaders had belonged to the parish previously. A deacon who was a parishioner in his parish for many years before his appointment as the pastoral administrator explained how he dealt with identity problems:

> I think probably half of them [parishioners] really respect what I do. I guess because I've been there so long, they know what I can do, and what I can't do. Their kids call me Deacon, they call me Father, some of them call me by my first name. That's fine, I'm a father, too.

One bishop said that he had reflected on the diaconate over a period of years, and he disagreed with the idea that "the whole reason for the permanent diaconate was to pick up the slack when there aren't priests." He continued,

> I am not one of those who thinks that permanent deacons should be there in place of the priest who can't be there. But they should assist, as they always have. Maybe part of the problem is that we got too much into the idea that permanent deacons are liturgical ministries only, and not ministries of service to the larger population. So I don't think having a permanent deacon head a parish is necessarily a help. I think it could be a hindrance. When they went through the diaconate program, they weren't trained to do that kind of parish work.

It is important to keep in mind that not all deacons have the training or the authority to preach during Mass. A bishop explained, "We have ordained deacons who do not have faculties to preach, and ordained deacons who do have faculties to preach."

A bishop said that if he had a choice between a deacon and a layman to head a parish, he would choose a deacon because he can baptize and preside at marriage ceremonies and at funerals, whereas a layman cannot do so as readily. This bishop was located in a diocese growing in membership due to high immigration rates, and he was particularly concerned about priest burnout. So he favored deacons heading parishes because that "alleviates the need for a priest to baptize."

Deacons have some restrictions with regard to the right to administer the sacraments. If they are parish leaders they can bring viaticum to dying parishioners and officiate at funerals outside of Mass and at burial services. In spite of their clerical state and their close connection to their parishioners, the parish leaders who are deacons do not have the right to administer the sacrament of the anointing of the sick. One of the deacons described a situation when he was called to the bedside of a parishioner. When he arrived, the person was already dead. The deacon explained,

> They wanted the anointing, and I called and Father said he's not going to come in the middle of the night for a dead person. He just said for me to say some prayers, so that's what I did and the family seemed to be fine about that.

This constraint regarding the anointing of the sick came up in some of my interviews with bishops. One of them explained that some of the bishops asked Pope John Paul II for his permission to allow deacons to anoint the sick when parishioners are dying. But, as he carefully worded it, "The pope would not allow that as an option."

The same constraint applies to the sacrament of reconciliation, or confession. One of the visiting priests explained that a deacon does not have the faculties to hear confessions. As he described it, a deacon "could pray with them, but he couldn't absolve." This constraint also applies in a sudden death situation with no priest available. In order to prepare people for such a situation, the priest explained that he always tells people, "Any time you say you're sorry, you're forgiven."

One of the deacons talked about a similar problem he encountered when there was no priest available:

> There was one guy who really poured his heart out to me, a lot of trouble, drugs and everything else, and I did pray with him and I suggested that when he got a chance that he see a priest and go to confession. I remember him saying, "Well, why do I have to go to a priest when I've already poured my heart to you and you're God's representative? Are you telling me that

God didn't hear me?" And I tried to encourage him to go to confession [to a priest], because what I had done didn't give him the grace of the sacrament. And I don't think the fellow ever went.

A female parishioner said, "The title [Deacon] definitely helps." To which a male parishioner added, "I think the ordination brings with it the authority that people in Catholicism look for."

In stark contrast to the discussions regarding authority and titles was the view presented by a Hispanic deacon about his work as a "calling:"

If I had my choice I probably wouldn't be ordained a priest. I'd remain a deacon. I'm like this with the Lord. I tell him not to give me too much fame because it might go to my head. Don't give me too many riches because they might separate me from him. Some people have asked me, "When did you feel a call to serve the church, and when did you start preparing for this? And I tell them, "From the day I was born. Every single thing that has ever happened to me in my life has had a meaningful purpose to touch other people's lives. Whether it's been driving a Caterpillar, an earth mover, driving a car, a tractor trailer, a crop duster, whatever. It's been a ministry, ministering to others."

Similarly, an African American deacon described himself as a bridge, in contrast to the image of a deacon's title as a badge. He said that he wore an alb and stole during Mass, because it was a requirement, and he explained the difference between the priest and himself:

First of all, I'm a family member. Also, I'm a bridge between the priest and their sacramental ministry, and

the lay people....Wearing a Roman collar would disas-
sociate myself from my relationship to the lay people. I
was certainly one of them, and I'm still one of them, in
heart, in action, in everything else. Until it comes to
ministry. Then I am the deacon.

The wife of a deacon said the parishioners still saw her husband as a married person, not as clergy, and that some people even
refused to receive communion from him at Mass. In fact, during
communion time they would switch aisles in order to receive communion from the priest. She also stated that some of the people
that her husband visited who were sick or shut in refused to receive
holy communion from him when he arrived at the house. She
described it as an "eye-opening" experience for both of them.

Lay Leaders: Constraints and Opportunities

Now picture yourself sitting in another Catholic church during a Sunday Mass. When the priest clad in his vestments enters
from the back of the church, he is preceded by two teenaged altar
servers, one male and one female, and a man dressed in a suit and
tie who walks directly in front of the priest. When they reach the
altar, it is the layman who steps to the microphone to greet the
parishioners and introduce newcomers to the congregation. After
that he moves to a chair on the side of the altar where he remains
until the priest sits down after reading the Gospel. At that point
the layman approaches the priest, kneels down to receive his
blessing, and then proceeds to the pulpit, where he delivers the
sermon. You notice some smiles on parishioners' faces when he
brings in examples from his life at home with his wife and children
to illustrate some of the lessons in the scripture readings. At the
conclusion of the sermon, he bows to the priest, and returns to his
chair at the side of the altar, until time for the kiss of peace, when

together they walk down the main aisle, shaking hands and greeting the parishioners in the pews. At communion time the layman also assists the priest in distributing the hosts.

After Mass is over, the layman joins the priest in processing to the door of the church, and both of them greet the parishioners outside the church. You may notice that the parishioners refer to the layman by his first name, but they are careful to use the title "Father," when speaking to the priest or when referring to him. You can't help but notice that there is a teenager who calls him Daddy, and a woman beside him holding the teenager's hand. You also notice that the lay man seems to be more familiar with the names of the parishioners than the priest, so you sneak another look at the church bulletin and note the titles "visiting priest" and "pastoral administrator." That solves the mystery. You are in a parish where there is no resident priest, and the head of the parish is a married layman.

As I previously mentioned, ordination can be described as a class or status position in the church. Those who belong to the ordained status (bishops, priests, and deacons) are placed in a category of authority, while the laity (married and single nonordained men and all married and single women) are situated in a nonauthoritative position in the church.

The advertisement for a pastoral administrator position from a Catholic paper mentioned earlier lists as a requirement a minimum of bachelor's degree, a degree or certificate in theology, pastoral ministry, or the equivalent. Some of the dioceses also require a master's degree in theology, religion, pastoral studies, or related fields. Administrative experience is often mentioned in these ads as well. Recall that the lay leaders included in this study tended to be more highly educated than the deacons.

Nonetheless, a layman is more restricted in his pastoral duties because he lacks the credentials of ordination. As one of the bishops explained with regard to baptisms,

Whenever possible baptism takes place within the Eucharist, and since the priest is required for the anointing as part of the ritual, we have said that normally that is done by the priest with the parish director being very much a part of the ritual. The parish director has the faculty to baptize in emergencies. If the priest doesn't show up, the parish director can do it. But the requirement, canonically and rubrically, is that then the priest supplies the ceremony some other time, because that includes the anointing with chrism.

A female parishioner stated that her experience with a lay pastor "has helped people realize that God can inspire lay people as well as clergy." She spoke these words with great intensity, and added, "The experience with his leadership is a real strength. It's not just the priests that can be inspired, but it's lay people who can be inspired, too."

One of the lay leaders talked about a constraint regarding the anointing of the sick that he shared with deacons heading parishes:

The only sticking point, and I don't think this is any different with a deacon, is not being an ordinary minister of the anointing of the sick. And so even in that circumstance, you could be walking with a person through a serious illness, and neither one of us is granted faculties to anoint. If a person is going to die, you're [deacons and laity] not supposed to anoint. And if [the dying person] were capable, I would do the viaticum. That's well within my rights and duties. If, for instance, they were going to go into surgery, and the surgery was life threatening, and there was just no way to get a priest there, I would pray over them, and I would lay hands on them.

A layman described how he avoided the symbols of hierarchy when he presided over a Sunday word and communion service:

> One Sunday the snow was so bad, and [the assisting priest] said, "I'm not going to make it over [to the church]." Some of the parishioners came on snowmobiles. I presided, but I was wearing my suit....That's how I would dress when I was on a parish staff as a liturgist. Now I've had one parishioner [who saw me wearing an alb once] who said, "I liked you in that alb. You should do that more often." But I don't like me in that alb. I don't want to be perceived as different from [other laymen]. Even the bishop suggested that maybe I should wear an alb, and he said, "Well, you know it's the baptismal garment."
>
> Yeah, it is, but then put it on everybody, and then I'll wear one. I have this thing, from a liturgist perspective, that the protocol of our liturgy is still imperialistic. We bow. It's a court liturgy. The whole protocol and even the vesture tends to separate the presiding minister from the assembly, and therefore creates a division and a distinction that ought not to be. We're all baptized, and there is no longer Jew or Greek, and if you want to push this, then give everybody an alb when they come into church, and we'll all wear them.

A lay parish leader gave a brief and clear rationale regarding his vocation as a layperson: "I haven't considered the diaconate. I haven't felt the call to that, which would be even kind of a middle step, if you will. It's a call to orders."

His wife said that her husband would probably be more acceptable if he had been a deacon, but she hastened to say that it was only a "guess" on her part. She continued, "But all in all, he was very accepted by the parishioners, which was a surprise, considering it's an older parish and older people. So maybe being a deacon would have helped a little iota more, but not substantially."

A male parishioner ranked his lay leader's sermons "as good as a lot of priests I've heard." He also expressed positive sentiments about the role of deacon. With regard to the other parishioners, he predicted,

> Some people would accept him more…to keep our small parish going. That's what's important. But the American people don't have too much contact with deacons to begin with…what they do and can't do. Now my brother's a priest in New Guinea, and they're twenty years ahead of us. He gets to a parish once a month. And they have their lay catechists who take care of the parish when [the priest] is gone.

A parishioner whose pastor was a married deacon offered her reflections regarding the acceptance of a nonclerical leader:

> I believe it all depends on how the person will conduct himself. If a layperson will be doing what [he] is doing as a deacon, I don't think he would be seen differently, because he's living the life you expect. That's how we see it: a dedicated person who is there one hundred percent of the time to meet his responsibilities.

Another group of parishioners with a lay leader expressed little or no ambivalence about their situation. They were strongly supportive of their lay leader, in particular because he was "on the same level" as they were. When I introduced the issue of ordination to the diaconate, a parishioner said, "I think we might lose what we said before, of being on the same level. Because the deacons have been trained very much like the clerics. It's that clerical office again."

Another parishioner in the same group said this about her pastor:

> In the mornings, when I'm going to work, I always pray, going down the highway, for safety and all. And one thing I always put in is, I say, "Lord, be good to my pastor and my church." I'm always saying "Pastor" when I pray for him.

A bishop stated that the chief role of the layperson is as a "leaven in society." He said that there is "an important place for laypersons in roles of leadership and governance within the church that enhances the quality of the church's mission, because they bring expertise that we do not have." He gave a personal example: his own lack of expertise in finance. Therefore, he said that he needed to "depend upon a lay person who's an expert in the area of finance." And he concluded by stating, "So in those areas it's important that there be lay leadership."

A female parishioner invoked Vatican II in the description of her parish:

> The advantage is to get away from that clerical attitude that people have had in the past, that you have to have a priest or cleric in charge of a parish. And it moves more into what I believe Vatican II is all about, that lay people are the people who should be really in charge of the parish in the sense of owning it. My own experience early on was the priest owned the parish. He made all the decisions. We've moved away from that.

A male parishioner also told me that it was because he and his wife had been "schooled in a strong sense of lay ministry" that they decided to join the parish. He said that they were also attracted by the dynamism of the layman's preaching the first time they heard him, and he added, "When we found out that there was not going to be a resident sacramental minister, we wanted to be more involved, and it was pretty apparent that this was a collaborative parish."

Another parishioner elaborated on this layman's leadership. She said,

> [He] is very much into gathering and community. And any time we have a small gathering where everyone can get up around the altar, he invites that. He wants to get away from that separation of the priest up here and the lay people down there. We all feel a bigger part of this parish.

Because a lay leader has no official ecclesiastical title, there was some confusion regarding what to call him in these parishes. "Reverend" or "Father," titles used for priests, and "Deacon" or "Reverend Mr.," titles for deacons, cannot be used for laymen. One of the wives, who was located in a new parish community in the deep South, said that most of the parishioners referred to her husband by his first name, but that some of them had used "Father." She said, "Most people would probably introduce him as 'Pastor,' or 'minister' or 'preacher.' That's a big one down here, you know. Some of them might say, 'He's our preacher.'"

The assisting priest in that same community said that the title he used differed, depending on the audience:

> If I'm in a Catholic circle, I'll call him a "pastoral coordinator." Sometimes, when I'm talking to people, I'll call him a "lay missionary." If I'm talking to Baptist-type folks, he's a "church planter." That's a Baptist term, meaning he plants a new church. Often I'll call him a "lay pastor." But I'm not consistent.

A parishioner in another parish, referring to her own pastoral administrator, stated:

> It seems to me like it would be nice to have some official way to, I don't know if ordain is the right word, but to officially include people in [his] position, because it seems there's a need for that. I think it would be nice if he had some way to be more recognized, like a deacon.

When discussing his parishioners' attitude toward his own lay state, a lay leader said,

> A couple of times a year, some people will say, "It would be great if you'd be ordained a deacon." Sometimes I almost feel like saying to them, "Is it that you'd feel better or because I'd feel better?" My sense overall is that they'd feel better because at least I'd be ordained up front. I prefer to be lay because I think that symbolically it's better to show that a nonordained person can function very well in this role.

One of the objections that has been raised about the appointing of married men to head parishes is the possible detriment to the stability of their marriages. Like doctors and counselors, pastors are expected to put in many hours on the job, and to be accessible outside of official hours in case of grave illness. The typical Catholic priest is viewed as one who should be available to serve his parishioners for counseling and for administering the sacraments of anointing of the sick or baptism in case of grave need any time of the day or night. Indeed, one of the arguments for celibacy is that having a wife and children would make a priest less accessible. It is also argued that the accessibility requirement would work against a stable family life, especially if the marriage were in its early stages. In this respect it is important to remind the reader

that not one of the men in my study could be described as a new-
lywed. In fact, all of the parish leaders in this study share the marital status of the majority of their adult parishioners, and this
similarity serves as a bridge between the visiting priest and the
members of the parish.

A male parishioner described his deacon as standing "in the
same shoes as we are":

> He hasn't been insulated the way that a priest is insu-
> lated from his parishioners, just because of his back-
> ground. He appreciates what we contend with daily as
> parishioners. Because the deacon is married and he has
> a budget, he knows how we're struggling with our
> household budget, more than our priests used to,
> because everything was taken care of for them.
> Whereas [our deacon] is in the same shoes as we are.
> He has to pay his insurance, his car…

The deacons also viewed their marital status as a facilitating
factor for their leadership in the parish. The fact that they were
married and brought their wives and children with them to the
parish was unlike anything the parishioners had ever experienced.

A Mexican American deacon, who was overwhelmed when
asked to head a parish, described his decision-making process:

> So I spent a lot of time in prayer. I spent a lot of time
> talking to my family, seeing what they thought and felt
> about my doing this. I talked to my boss at work because
> taking this assignment was going to impact on my work.

He then presented his reasons for accepting the assignment:

> I accepted it because I think that's what God was calling
> me to do. I really do. After a lot of prayer and talking to

people, there were lots of times that I thought what the Church would be like under a different structure. That it should be more of a "family-type" structure, versus someone really being over the parish rather than working with it, and I said, "Wow!" This was a perfect opportunity for a parish of this type to really blossom and find itself.

Like the parishioners in my study of parishes headed by women, some of these parishioners did not embrace their new leader at first, because they were in the midst of grieving at the loss of their priest. They also viewed themselves as "second-class citizens" compared to most of the parishes in the diocese, because they no longer had a resident priest as their pastor.

One of the deacons who came from another location described how some of the parishioners reacted on his arrival at the parish:

Initially, when I started interacting with parishioners, everybody kind of kept their arm's length. They were very careful what they said. At that point I said, "Who do you think I am, a monk, or what? I'm not. I'm married. Hey, I like to cut up like anybody else." So eventually that was eroded. Being a family member and a father and a husband allows me a bit greater access to the families in a much more personal way.

One of the lay leaders spoke with a sense of awe when he described his present occupation as "a dream come true." He said,

When people ask me about this position, it goes back to my college seminary days of dreaming and thinking about the priesthood seriously, but also realizing that

I wasn't ready for a lifelong commitment at that time, and not sure about celibacy and marriage…but wanting to be in ministry and in a parish. It's kind of like a dream come true, being married and being in a pastor position. So it kind of came full circle, and it's just, you know, to be in the middle of a group of people who are trying to pave the road to the kingdom and create the kingdom here on earth, it's really powerful to be a part of that.

Another lay leader viewed his marital status as a facilitating factor because he can empathize with his married parishioners:

I'm able, from experience, to assure them that even good people have these kinds of thoughts or behaviors in a normal married life. One time I called up this couple, and I definitely got them at a bad time. They were in a real honker of an argument. I was able to say, "I understand it's a kind of a bad time right now. I'll call back in about a half hour, okay?" So when I was at their house I was able to say, "So you guys fight, too, eh?" And was able to laugh with them about it. I said, "I don't know how many times [my wife] and I have gone through that. We just think the roof is going to cave in." So I'm able to empathize with them and to reduce the sense of embarrassment or even shame about these things

The priest, who worked with this man as his sacramental minister, said that the married leader had a better understanding of people's way of life, and that he could connect better with them than a priest could. He used his preaching as an example when he said, "His reflections during his sermons bring in some of those human experiences in marriage better than I can."

Speaking about the advantage of married life for parish leaders, a parishioner pointed to another aspect of his role, as counselor to his parishioners. She said, "I think it helps him, especially in marriage counseling. I've always felt, 'How can you really talk to a priest about being married, because he's never been there?'"

Race, Ethnicity, and Gender Issues

Given the increasing numbers of Catholic Hispanics in the United States, men like the Mexican American deacon quoted earlier, are an important resource. Even though these men are lower order clergy, the services they are able to perform by virtue of their ordination are helpful for the continuing existence of virtually all of the parishes where they are the leaders.

All five of the nonwhite and non-Anglo pastoral administrators mentioned racism as an issue for them. One of the Mexican American deacons said, "The barrio church, unfortunately, was created for the purpose of segregation, and keeping the classes separate." He also spoke of the racial separation among deacons, and quoted Hispanic priests who "feel the separateness that exists, even in their own brotherhood of priests, between the Anglo priests and the Hispanic priests." He said that a two-day diocesan clergy conference where priests and deacons come together to discuss a variety of topics, typically deacons sat with deacons, and priests sat with priests, and the Anglo deacons and Hispanic deacons sat separately.

On the other hand, this same deacon described a supportive action on the part of an Anglo priest. This priest phoned him to say that a couple had come to him to have their marriage validated, but the priest did not speak Spanish, and he asked the deacon if he would come to his parish and validate the marriage. As he described this ceremony, the deacon emphasized that it was the priest, who, rather than standing by like a spectator, took the role of the altar server. The deacon was astounded that an ordained priest took the altar boy's position. The deacon said he was overwhelmed by this role reversal. He also said he felt uncomfortable because he had never had a priest on the altar with him who took a lower position. Then slowly and carefully he pronounced these words: "He treated me as his EQUAL!"

A bishop also spoke to the issue of discrimination and segregation between the Anglos and Hispanics, and the importance of having native leadership, like the Mexican American leader whom he had appointed to head a parish:

> In some towns you find two cemeteries: one for the Anglos and one for the Hispanics. Or one cemetery, but one area for the Anglos and one for the Hispanics. Or in some towns you'll find two Catholic churches: one with 120 families and one with almost 700 families. And I'll let you guess which is which. So, in this kind of context, the native leadership in that native context makes a big difference. And his experience as a husband and father enables him to bring an intuition of pastoral insight, a quality of ministry that can enhance his work among the people.

For me, the question about the suitability of deacons with less formal education faded into the background when I visited the poor nonwhite parishes that were headed by African American, Hispanic, or Native American married men. The fact that these deacons were of the same racial and ethnic background as their parishioners was a key factor for the strong solidarity that was evident in these parishes. This was especially so when I listened to them as they preached, and observed the verbal and nonverbal reactions of their congregations.

One of those moments occurred in a poor barrio on the outskirts of the city in a Mexican American parish that was headed by a Mexican American deacon with a high school education. At the conclusion of his sermon, I witnessed something seldom heard during a Catholic Mass: a wave of spontaneous and prolonged applause. This particular deacon reminded me of Saint Jean Vianney, the patron saint of parish priests, who was a renowned and dearly loved priest, and like his parishioners, he came from a poor family in rural France.

One of the parishioners in this Mexican American parish said this about his pastor:

> He gives very good homilies. He makes you feel like we can do something about changing our lives. He gives us examples from his own life, the way it's supposed to be. He tells things without hairs on his tongue. He talks straight, even if it hurts him sometimes.

This deacon was the only one of the Mexican American deacons in his diocese who was appointed to head a parish. He admitted that many of these deacons called him for advice from time to time, and he spoke to me about his efforts to create a community among his fellow deacons. He said,

> I have tried to establish some kind of support group with the Hispanic deacons, but for some reason we just never were able to set one up. I would love to have a support group of all the Hispanic deacons. Just to build community and to find out how things are working. I'm working on something right now.

Prior time in the parish did not help in the case of a deacon who was appointed as the parish leader after having spent years of outreach service in the community. In my interview with the parishioners of this parish, one of them suggested an important strategy on the part of the bishop that might have helped all con-cerned if it had occurred at the time of the deacon's appointment:

> When this happens there should be a meeting with the [diocesan leader] who comes to the church and says, "This deacon is running this property. These are his responsibilities." Because the congregation doesn't realize it, and they haven't had this before, they don't know how to accept the deacon as the head of the parish. And that's the reason for the turmoil we're going through.

A white deacon, who was the pastoral administrator in a predominantly African American neighborhood, had difficulties from the beginning because the parishioners were given no clear explanation of his role. In fact, the visiting priest said that there was a "minor rebellion" when the parishioners discovered the identity of their new leader, because they wanted a priest. And, he added,

> If the bishop had come and helped with the transition, that might have been better, but the mistakes were made, and they were inadvertent. Like the first meeting with the council, [the pastoral administrator] got angry with them and told them it was his church.
>
> Those were his words: "It was his church." They went bananas. It's not his church. He's in charge of the church. But it's not his church. See, that just set them off.... But finally the bishop did come down there and met with all of us and did talk to [the pastoral adminis-trator], and told him that he just needed to be discreet, and use discretionary powers about certain things. So things worked themselves out.

In fact this kind of meeting was very helpful for both the parishioners and the new leaders I interviewed in my earlier study of Catholic parishes headed by women. As we will see in chapter 7, some of the bishops made an effort to visit the parish prior to the arrival of the new leader, and, while there, conducted an open meeting with the parishioners. The bishops usually took this opportunity to explain the rationale for this new type of leadership. They also clarified the extent of the new leader's responsibilities, and invited the parishioners to ask questions before the conclusion of the session. This meeting not only served to "pave the way" for the new leader, but it also alleviated some of the anxiety of parishioners who, up to this point, had always had a priest as pastor of their parish.

Although the deacons and laymen had to deal with constraints in their work as parish leaders due to the limits on their sacramental privileges, there were benefits to all concerned when the man in charge shared the racial or ethnic characteristics of their parishioners.

The issue of gender differences also came up when a bishop told about a series of consultations about starting a diaconate training program in one of the dioceses. He said that the priests were generally not in favor of it, and this bishop discussed a key issue regarding priorities of resources:

> If we're going to start the diaconal training program, then that means we're going to put a lot of energy, finances, and so on into that, and then we won't be able to develop the lay ministry formation program. The second thing was that women would be excluded, and that would be a problem....So we decided not to go ahead with it. Still, people will come and say, "I feel called to the diaconate. How come you won't allow me to fulfill my vocation?" So there's a point to that, too, like women

who feel called to ordination….So there would be some
value to ordaining pastoral administrators, at least those
who feel called to diaconal ministry, especially those who
emphasize diaconal ministry, reaching out to the poor,
the sick, and other social concerns.

The wife of a layman who was copastoring with her husband
in a small town in the deep South said,

I couldn't be a deacon. Also, in some ways, in the
[teachings of the] Baptist church, I'm not on an equal
par with my husband. One of the things that we struggle with here is that the non-Catholic faiths see me as
his wife, not the copastor. So they will ask him to speak
[in their church].

Her husband added,

And that's ingrained in the culture. They almost assume
there's nothing else possible. I made a conscious decision not to become a deacon. As long as they wouldn't
ordain her as a deacon, I didn't want to be ordained.

Another lay leader offered these reflections:

We have a friend who is a deacon. His wife highly
resented the way women were treated when he was
going through the deacon program. As a wife of a deacon, she felt very second-rate.

A lay leader used the term "uncomfortable" when he
expressed his feelings on the topic of the diaconate. He said,

I'm not real comfortable overall with the diaconate at
this point where they only allow men. So it almost

seems better to me to stay where I'm at, because to me, the diaconate is this in-between thing that the retired men do. I mean, that's what it's evolved to, and it has this kind of fuzzy liturgical role. I'd feel a little uncomfortable if some of my women counterparts couldn't become deacons, but "I'm going to do it." And so I kind of stay where I'm at, I guess.

Collaborative Leadership: Deacons

The Latin verb *collaborare*, means "to labor together." Working jointly with others is at the heart of collaborative leadership, and collaborative leaders will tend to opt for sharing authority in the decision-making process, rather than keeping it as their own prerogative. I have often quoted one of the women pastors in my first parish study when I speak on this topic:

> Leadership is listening to parishioners' initiatives. A leader listens and then articulates the needs and direction of the community, and finds ways to name it and facilitate it. The most valuable thing I think anybody could have who would find themselves in this position [as parish leader] would be to maintain their sense of deep respect for all of the people that you work with, and not think that you are in a position of authority over them. That's not what being a parish leader is about.[7]

Needless to say, leadership was a topic of great interest to parishioners, bishops, and the leaders themselves in this study of married male leaders. For instance, a Hispanic deacon described how he approached the leadership issue with his parishioners:

After I took over, I said, "Folks, you need to take ownership of the parish. Its successes, its failures, cannot lie on one person. It lies on each and every one of us, because we are all baptized and called to those ministries. If [our parish] is going to be vibrant and lifegiving, it's not going to be because of Father…and me. We may facilitate some of that, but it's up to you to take charge."

A parishioner in this parish discussed his new leader's impact:

I think he's brought a lot of involvement within the parish. He always gets the parishioners involved in the decisions. When it comes to expenditures, he'll say, "Well, what do you think? What are our priorities?" What he does is, he gets input from the parishioners to prioritize the needs of the church.

A female parishioner who was a member of the parish council in another parish headed by a deacon said,

I think that if people don't voice their own opinions, it's their own fault, because we have asked for opinions. Questionnaires have been sent out. The meetings are open. We have a whole bunch of commissions that people can serve on. If they don't have a say, it's not because anybody has shut the door on them.

One of the parishioners in a Hispanic parish headed by a deacon explained the process for parishioner input:

If you have a concern, you can approach one of the council members and let them know. And if they feel your concern will be better understood by your making an appearance, you're allowed to go to the council meeting. It's not a hush-hush sort of thing.

An African American deacon told me how he introduced his parishioners to the concept of ownership, and the responsibility that stems from it:

> I think we all need to be part of that decision-making process, as happens in a family. And some of this needs to be designated, like in the parish council. In the beginning, you know, we had a lot of committees that were just there by name. When I came on board, I had this burst of energy, and it rallied around encouraging people to take ownership and encouraging people to be active. You know, I have this little cliché. And it is this: "If you give birth to an idea, then you are responsible for raising it."

He transmitted the concept of ownership to his parishioners by repeating his "little cliché" whenever it seemed appropriate. Several of his parishioners repeated the deacon's words to me with a great sense of conviction, illustrating that they not only understood it, but more importantly, that they had internalized the meaning of it as well.

The deacon's role in the parish council just mentioned is a good illustration of the collaborative leadership model. He explained that he was the one who called the meetings of the council and drew up the agenda for them. When I asked him about the voting process, his answer was, "I don't vote. I let them make the decisions." He then elaborated:

> What I've tried to do is to change the style of leadership to empower people: ownership, responsibility, and accountability. When I grew up in the church, the pastor figure was one of dominance, of control. I've tried to

undo that structure....We're too "Catholic" in the sense that one waits for direction versus one taking direction. Kind of like my military experience where they would ask you to check your brain in, so you don't think. When I was growing up in the church, we didn't allow people to be creative, to use their skills and talents. The Father-did-it-all-type concept. It was a dependency, and it's really hard to get people to recognize that they, too, have skills and talents.

A Mexican American deacon stressed the concept of working with, rather than for the parishioners:

The majority, particularly the fifty and sixty year olds, even the late forty year olds, looked at the priest like a doctor or lawyer. You know, you have them, but you really don't use them until you need them. So that's a comfortable situation for them. With my role, I've made it very clear that I'm not here to do the work for them, but with them. So, in essence, I've had to force them to make them an integral part of the church. And make them see their responsibilities.

A parishioner in a parish headed by a Hispanic deacon also used the term "ownership":

I think all of us have become more involved within our parish. Being here seventeen years, I would say it's in the last three years that I have really become active. Before that if I was asked to do something, I would do it. Where now, I really feel that we have ownership. We know that if we don't give our time and talents, that this parish is not going to run. We can't expect [our deacon] to carry the whole burden. So I feel all of us have become more active.

One strategy to encourage the parishioners' ownership of the parish was graphically described by a parish leader who had a full-time job outside the parish. He explained that, since he was not living in the rectory, and thereby, "not accessible to folks twenty-four hours a day," his solution was to create a new role that he called the "keeper of the keys":

> In my current situation what I've done is given people keys who need keys. And so committee chairs or who- ever else needs access to the buildings are responsible for opening up and closing, and making sure things are in order when they leave. I just can't be everything for everybody, so there may be fifteen keys out in the parish, given to people who need access to the buildings.

He also described another instance when he transmitted the meaning of ownership. On this occasion a parishioner who was doing committee work at the rectory asked the deacon for permis- sion to use the telephone, and his reply was, "Why are you asking me to use your own phone? This is your house, not my house."

Several parishioners indicated that they valued their empow- erment. One of them, a female parishioner, expressed her senti- ments about ownership in this way:

> I think we all feel better knowing that we have a voice in whatever is going on. There are so many committees that are involving so many people. Nobody is left over in a corner somewhere.

One woman stated, "We are the church. The church is its people, not the priest, not the bishop, but its people." In a similar vein, a woman who was on a committee for renovations of the church reported that when they brought their recommendations to the parish council, the deacon was present, but he did not make the final decision on his own. She concluded, "I think there's more say now in the church than what it used to be."

A deacon reported that when he was appointed as parish leader there was no functioning parish council, and in fact there had been very little parishioner involvement in anything before he arrived, with the exception of the choir. Therefore, in addition to training parishioners for the roles of lector and eucharistic ministers at Mass, he and his parishioners had the task of drawing up the laws and constitution for their parish council.

A visiting priest compared the leadership of a Hispanic deacon as "incredibly more collaborative" than the former priest pastor. He said that the priest had "no structures of lay participation," and described the parish as "old style." He summed it up by saying this about the present parish leadership: "I think it's moving from a hierarchical to a much more collaborative style."

Another deacon described what he did when a strong division of opinion would arise among the parishioners at a parish council meeting. He said,

> I just gather them together. Both parties. And I put them in a prayer situation in our little Blessed Sacrament chapel. Preferably on a weekend or an evening when they're available. We join our hands and our minds and our whole being in prayer, and then I bring up the Gospel, and I say, "It can't be like that among you. You know how it is among the people of this world who are leaders. They lord it over their subjects. With you, if you are to be a leader, you have to be a servant." That's enough. They understand what I'm saying better than if I was just to use my own words.

In answer to my original question, "Were the deacons collaborative leaders?," the answer is "Yes, in all but two cases." One exception was a deacon in a predominantly African American parish who was an "outsider" on two counts: He was white, and lived outside the parish boundaries. In addition, the parishioners received no preparation from diocesan officials for this new form of parish leadership prior to his appointment.

The other exception was a white deacon who was also a "stranger," coming from a large urban parish to a small rural parish. From the day of his arrival he made it clear that all of the final decisions were his prerogative. As one of the parishioners described it, the parish committees always presented the facts and figures to the deacon, along with their proposals, but it was he who made the final decisions. As the parishioner explained, "The decision was ultimately his. Whether we liked it or whether we didn't like it, it was his decision."

One of the results of this deacon's authoritarian leadership style was a loss of parishioners. When I interviewed the visiting priest, he reported that he was aware that parishioners had been voting with their feet by joining other parishes. The priest voiced his concern when he said, "Good people are leaving there." In the last analysis the priest said he "felt sorry for him," but predicted that the deacon would probably leave within the year, because "another couple of years would just hurt him or the parish more." This priest, who was especially concerned because the deacon was isolating himself, said: "He's not reaching out and going to the meetings with the other pastoral leaders in the region."

All five of the nonwhite deacons were collaborative leaders, and they had "insider status" in their parish because their racial and ethnic characteristics were the same as their parishioners. Three of the white deacons who were recruited from inside the parish were also collaborative leaders. Only the two aforementioned white deacons could be classified as hierarchical leaders.

Thus, "insider status" as a former parishioner or as a member of the same racial or ethnic group as their parishioners was a facilitating factor for the practice of collaborative leadership by these married deacons.

Collaborative Leadership: Laymen

As we now turn our attention to the leadership styles of the laymen, keep in mind that all of the laymen were white, and on average they were more highly educated than the deacons. Unlike deacons, however, laymen cannot be placed on the lower end of the continuum of clerical privilege. There is, in fact, a clear dividing line between clergymen and laymen, so we will be shifting conceptually from a continuum to a dichotomy. Unlike deacons who are "outsiders within" because they have some clerical privileges, laymen are completely "outside the pale" of clerical privilege.[8]

A lay leader used the term "collaborative delegator" when he described his leadership role:

> I think it's a good title, "pastoral administrator." I would hope that as a layperson that I am an administrator who is a collaborative delegator, encouraging other people to play their rightful baptismal role in the parish. And last Lent we had different goal-setting groups that got together for four weeks in a row to set the goals and objectives. I could have done it myself and saved a lot of time, but that's the key area in leadership nowadays. We have to fight against that history in the Catholic Church of the priest making the decisions, of everybody following what Father says, instead of a communal model where we have a say in the decisions in the parish, and take more ownership.

An announcement in one of the parish bulletins described the characteristics necessary for nominations to the parish council. The parishioners were instructed to consider the following characteristics:

> People who you feel have leadership abilities that are rooted in their spirituality. People with a sense of what [our parish] is, and more importantly, a vision of what we are being called to become. People who are willing to give of their time and talent in a special way as a member of the parish council. The selection of parish leaders is not a race or contest, but a call.

A strategy that was used in several parishes was described to me as "a process of listening and dialogue, called the servant process." One lay parish leader said that in making any decision, like a building renovation, the first step for the building committee, which met weekly, was to look at all of the options. They also had a parish-wide survey to get a sense of how the parish as a whole viewed the project. As he explained, "It turned out that the option of fixing the roof was not an option" because of structural problems.

A parishioner described another lay leader's collaborative approach:

> He appointed a committee of parishioners and asked us to review the staffing and to make recommendations as to how it should be reorganized. What came out of it was a position that said we need someone who empowers the people and helps them to do what needs to be done. And I think that's a strong indication of our parish leader's collaborative approach to ministry. He listens to people and is willing to act on their suggestions. But most importantly he wants to move in the direction of lay leadership.

A lay leader described his leadership style as "going with the energy of the parish":

> I think people in the parish would say that they feel more connected to me than they have felt to the priest pastors. They feel a little more heard, maybe. So one thing I think I bring is I am connected with the people, and don't act without them. One thing we've talked about in the parish, and I think it's very true in the leadership style, is we go with the energy of the parish, what seems to be coming forth from the people, and what's the energy of those people. And that's where we've tended to put our time. My sense is that the priest pastors that I've worked with, and that would have been three of them, tended to come with a bit of their own agenda of things they thought were important in parishes. There's a bit of feeling [among parishioners] of getting an agenda imposed on them.

A lay leader described how he encouraged ownership among the parishioners:

> I try to build ownership, to [encourage] percolating up instead of trickling down. I think there's more power there,...a different model than people are used to. People are used to someone coming in and taking charge and saying, "This is the way it's going to be."

In most parishes, illustrations of encouraging parishioners to realize a sense of ownership can be found in the notices on bulletin boards and the pamphlets on tables set up just inside the door of the church. One of the pamphlets that I collected states, "You, the family of [parish name], are represented by the pastoral council. In order for us to meet your needs, we'd like to know your thoughts, concerns, and suggestions regarding all our parish activities. We would appreciate your written comments below. Remember, this is our parish, and only through you can we grow in Christ and in one another."

Another avenue is the church bulletin typically distributed in parishes each Sunday. In one parish, I noticed that the lay leader listed the name of each parishioner who had participated in recent parish projects by donating time or money. Naming people served as an "'Atta boy," as one of the parishioners described it to me. It was one of this leader's ways to thank or stroke people:

> I think it's just part of his charisma. Being able to get people to follow him and volunteer for things. He gives everybody an "'Atta boy." Next time he asks, it just makes you want to say, "Hey, I'll go ahead and do that." And it would be detrimental to leave out somebody's name, but I don't think that's been the case yet.

I asked these lay leaders to explain how they created the decision-making process in these parishes. One of them said he used a consensus model that he learned from studying the Quaker decision-making process. He described this process by giving an example from a recent meeting of the building committee: a proposal to make an alteration in the original plan on maintenance of the church roof in order to lower the expense.

> So what we do is we go around the circle and everybody kind of says where they're at with [the proposal]: "It makes me uncomfortable," or "I see the value of that," or "No, I really like [the present plan]." And then if there's a serious question, then we'll stop and we'll take a few minutes out for silent prayer. And then we'll go around the circle again, and everybody's saying "Yeah, yeah, yeah," but then somebody will say, "No, I think this will

happen." And we'll go around the room again, and it will change, dramatically. So we stay away from the voting, and ask, "Are we heading in the right direction?" or "Do you trust where the group is heading?" And sometimes people will say, "No." And that's that prophetic voice out there, and then we have to deal with that. So we ask, "What do we have to change to make you comfortable with moving in this direction." And after that they're asked to say, "I agree with it" or "I can live with it."

Another lay parish leader told me that if the group was deeply divided over an issue, he would ask the members of the group to take some time out for discernment, before they gathered again as a group. He instructed them to take a period of two weeks or even longer before their next meeting, in order to take time to meditate and pray over it, so that the group could come to some consensus over their positions on the question at hand. At the next meeting, if the stalemate continued, he would instruct them to take another break before they called a meeting again. If, at the final vote of the group with regard to this issue, all but one of them were of the same mind, the parish leader would then turn to the lone dissenter on the group's decision, and ask him or her this question: "But can you live with it?"

Whether the answer was affirmative or negative, those leaders who used this means of decision making in their parishes said that, in general, the discernment process made it possible for minority voters to leave the room with dignity. One of them gave the example of a woman in his parish who went to another parish for Sunday Mass shortly after the council's decision, but returned a few weeks later, and was still an active member of her parish when I visited there.

Statements regarding the decision-making process also came from parishioners. One of them said, "I don't think there are any decisions that [the parish leader] makes alone. It's always brought up in some way with a group of people."

Another parishioner stated,

> We usually try to do it through discernment, through discussion, allowing people to say what they feel about the issue. We have always tried to make sure that when an issue is coming, there is a written proposal for people to see beforehand, so that they can come up with their own feelings and opinions ready to go. It does not always work that way. The majority of reasons that things have come to council and we've had trouble with discernment is basically because it's a last minute thing. It's very emotional when there's nothing in writing ahead of time.

Because the discernment process requires a considerable amount of patience and caring on the part of all participants, it is critical that the leader be an exemplar of these virtues. A lay pastoral administrator, while describing what his present occupation meant to him, borrowed from the parable of the good shepherd. He said,

> It means being pastor...pastor as shepherd. All the implications of that parable. Walking with the flock, ahead of the flock, behind the flock....a real pastoral care. A loving care, a presence that they don't receive in any other way in our society.
>
> When I visit them in the hospital, for instance, they have a lot of medical people coming in, but nobody seems to care in a pastoral kind of way. And I don't mean that people aren't kind in the hospital, but they come in and do their technical thing, and they're gone. And people are left there, [saying to themselves]

"What's happened to me?" So I see that [visiting them in the hospital] as pastoring.

A lay leader said he saw his chief task as "bringing forth the gifts of the people in the community, to enable them to exercise their gifts." He explained,

> My sense is, I don't really have any particular wisdom on any particular topic, but I think it's all out there in the community. If I can kind of help people come forward with their gifts and maybe help them make use of their gifts, then that's the role of the leader. An example would be a gentleman who has a tremendous amount of energy to start a young adult ministry, which we do not have right now. But he's also maybe a bit too impulsive at times, and tends to take off too fast in certain directions. I would say my role as leader is to work with him and help him get it successfully going, but yet not stifle the energy and enthusiasm he brings.

A lay leader emphasized a key element that served as a linchpin for him: trust.

> I think it's an honor in the sense of the trust that the bishop puts in me to be here. But also, the people, in terms of their level of trust, and the things that they share in their lives, life and death situations, the ups and downs. That even though I'm not what they're used to, and I don't have a collar, they still seem to support and feel supported by me. That they look to me to help them get closer to God, which is kind of a scary piece, too, because I know I struggle with it in my own life. You know, sometimes it even seems to work. (laughs) But that's the power of the Spirit.

Summary

Because all of the lay leaders shared the same religious status as their lay parishioners, it was not surprising to find that, without exception, all ten laymen practiced collaborative leadership. Although all of the Hispanic, African American, and Native American parish leaders were deacons, they shared the same cultural heritage as their parishioners, and their clerical status was not a deterrent to collaborative leadership. All of these parish leaders, however, shared a key characteristic with the majority of their parishioners: their marital status. The powerful statement regarding his parish leader by one of the married parishioners, "He's one of us!" says it all.

Collaborative leadership is also enhanced in parishes with stewardship programs that stress the contribution of time, talent, and treasure (money) on the part of parishioners. Both stewardship programs and collaborative leadership are, in fact, bringing new life to Catholic parishes.[9]

Chapter 3

The Pastor's Wife:
"There Wasn't a Role Model"

It never occurred to me that family members should be included in my earlier study of Catholic parishes headed by women. The insights and experiences of the husbands and children of the married women who were parish leaders and their counterparts, the sisters who were living in the rectory with another member of their religious community, could have shed some light on those situations. This, then, is my first research project that includes data from interviews with spouses and children.

Few contemporary Roman Catholic women ever dreamed that they would someday find themselves married to a man in charge of a Catholic parish. As children, they learned that their parish priest was a "Father," who had no wife or children of his own, because of his vow of celibacy.

It is no wonder, then, that the wives in my study had no clear-cut expectations about how to go about doing the work of a pastor's wife when they arrived at their husband's parish. As one of them told me, "There wasn't a role model." Two wives mentioned that they had relatives or friends who were wives of Protestant ministers, but most of them had never met a woman whose husband was the head of a Catholic parish prior to her husband's appointment.

The support of one's spouse is, of course, essential for the person appointed to head a parish. This was carefully spelled out in one of the dioceses I visited, where the guidelines for a married candidate for the position of pastoral administrator reads: "A sound and stable family life, valid in the eyes of the Church, and in which there is no significant conflict between the candidate's proposed work as a pastoral leader and the best interests of his or her family, and in which his or her spouse is accepting of the candidate's proposed service, and supportive of it."

Although they had no role models, the lack of clarity about what was expected of these wives had some advantages for them. They were, in fact, helping to create their own participation in this new social reality: a Catholic pastor's wife.

A Profile of the Twenty Wives

When I interviewed these women in 1996–97, the average age of the twenty wives was forty-nine, ranging from the youngest, who was twenty-six to the two oldest, who were sixty. Two were in their thirties, eight in their forties, and seven in their fifties. Clearly these were not young and inexperienced women. Ethnically and racially they mirrored their husbands: fifteen were white Americans of European ancestry, three were Mexican American, one was African American, and one was Native American. Thirteen of these women had some college experience, compared to seventeen of the husbands with similar experience. Two of the thirteen women had taken some college courses without finishing the degree; six had B.A.s, four had M.A.s, and one had a Ph.D. Thus, these women were only slightly less educated than their husbands.

One of the arguments presented against married clergy is that married men cannot afford to accept the job of parish administrator because the salary would not be sufficient to support his family. That argument rests on the assumption that this will be a "one paycheck" marriage with the wife working at home full time as parent and housekeeper, and the parish cannot afford a salary large enough to support a family. In the previous chapter, however, we saw that the majority of the men working full time in the parish were not receiving poverty-level salaries. What needs to be added to this picture, then, are their wives' financial contributions to the family.

Seventeen of the twenty wives were wage earners: nine were full-time workers and eight worked part-time. Only one wife worked full time for the parish, as a receptionist. The other full-time occupations included: public high school principal, public high school computer training specialist, parochial high school science teacher, public high school counselor for special education students, public grammar school teacher, telecommuter for a business firm, administrator for a national association, and medical secretary. The eight wives who were part-time wage earners worked as nurse, salesperson, librarian, grammar school teacher, office receptionist, copastor, bookkeeper, and parish receptionist. It is important to note that all but one of the seventeen women working outside the home described their jobs as meaningful.

Only three of the families could be described as "one pay-check" families. Two of these three wives were, in effect, donating their time and talent to the parish, and the other was a mother with five young children at home.

The eight wives who were working full time outside the parish also tended to donate some of their time and talents to the parish as volunteers. Since twelve of the households were "empty nests," they tended to spend some of their time helping out in the parish. However, four of the women with full-time jobs outside the parish said that they participated as parishioners in their husband's parish, but they had made a conscious decision to refrain from holding a parish leadership position. Three of these wives had very demanding jobs, and one who was working part time had two preschool children at home.

When I asked the sixteen who were parish volunteers what services they donated to the parish, most mentioned multiple services. Seven said they were eucharistic ministers; six were teachers in the religious education programs; four were involved in music ministry as choir directors or organists; four were in charge of the weekly bulletin; three each served as receptionists, lectors during Mass, and visitors to the sick and dying. Other work included committee work for social justice concerns, food pantry, liturgy, youth, helping in the business office, cleaning and renovating the church, and cooking for church functions.

Only two of the wives could be accurately described as working full time for the church without pay, and thereby engaging in the "two for the price of one" syndrome typical of Protestant churches until the advent of the contemporary women's movement. Because eighteen of the twenty Catholic wives in my study were not burdened with the "two for one" expectation, they were free to contribute their time and energies elsewhere.

Given their talents, one can only speculate about the degree of deprivation experienced by the society at large had all of these women been expected to work alongside their husbands in the parish. One was a nurse who was especially gifted in caring for victims of Alzheimer's disease. Her husband described an occasion when she accompanied him on a hospital visit to one of his parishioners, a woman who was critically ill. This was the first time he had witnessed his wife with family members at a deathbed, and he shed some tears toward the end of his testimony:

> She knew what they were talking about. She was just wonderful with that family. She walked with that family through the death of their parent. She's just awesome in it. She was just the person they needed.

I have used this particular instance to illustrate the general characteristics of the wives in my study: mature, well-trained women, most of whom had already been contributing their talents to organizations and communities outside the home before their husband's appointment. The husband's narrative reveals how the volunteer work of these wives constituted an important resource for these parishes. The issues that these women raised with me about their new role included the following: the visibility factor, roles for pastors' wives, financial and health issues, support groups, and views about the future.

Expectations and Early Experiences: The Visibility Factor

Some occupational roles, like that of pastor, carry with them high visibility, because most of the person's work is done in front of an audience: actors, highly placed political officials, athletes, broadcasters, and teachers. Sometimes a pastor's wife, like a politician's wife, is expected to be present at certain events where her spouse is "performing." In some circumstances her very absence is seen as a lack of support and this can be detrimental to her husband's success in the job.[1] She can, in effect, be a key player in the performance of his job. Recall, for instance, how often the camera shifts to the spouse during televised athletic contests or major speeches of noteworthy people.

In the parish situation, a pastor's wife can find herself on unfamiliar turf, and at times either unsure or ambivalent about how she is expected to act. One of the pastor's wives described her experience:

> You definitely lose anonymity. You are thrown in one hundred percent. There's a certain scrutiny that I was very aware of. It's just that you are suddenly in the lime-light. I felt very aware of how I dressed, very aware of how our children behaved in church. I remember when my youngest daughter sometimes would fuss, and I would think, "Oh gosh, I don't want them to think that the pastor's wife is being disruptive."

To avoid the stress of the "limelight effect" one of the wives, a part-time worker who has three children in grammar school, described a strategy she used prior to the move to the parish: talking about the parish with the sister who was the previous pastoral administrator. She explained her rationale:

> I insisted on talking to sister…because I was so unsure of what I was getting into. Although I know it was just my husband's job, I was uprooting my life. I wanted to know about the area, about the people. I wanted to know about the living conditions [in the rectory] and about the school system.

She also scrutinized the parochial school nearest to her husband's parish, and found it very small and limited, compared to the parochial school her children had been attending in the city. So on arrival at the parish she enrolled her children in a public school. She said that she subsequently experienced a "lot of flack" from some of the parishioners, who thought her children should attend the parochial school. However, this wife was not inclined to surrender to the parishioners' expectations. In fact, she told me that she thought it wasn't any of the parishioners' business to concern themselves about the choice of her children's school. Her children's positive experience in the previous school and her status as an out-of-towner influenced her stance regarding the parishioners' criticisms.

The adjustment process was qualitatively different for one of the wives whose family owned a home in another parish where she continued to work full time as a teacher in their parochial school. Her son explained,

> It was hard for my mom at first. She supported him emotionally, but our parish was right here, where we all grew up. Change is hard for my mom. This is the only

house that they've ever bought. Dad had one job for years and years. We were all baptized at our parish and went to the school, and Mom was involved in the choir. It seems like it took her a year or two before she really became actively involved in my dad's parish.

His mother explained to me how she and her husband went about "breaking new ground" for future pastor's wives:

Being removed from [his] rectory, I am not called upon to be the hostess of the parish, which is what I had anticipated having to be. That whenever there is any kind of function, I would have to be the hostess and [my husband] would be the host. That has not come to pass. I have not had that pushed on me at all. [My husband] has been very careful that I am not asked to do those kinds of things; that it's his job and not mine.

The expectations of the parishioners were particularly difficult at the beginning of the new leader's work in the parish. One wife said,

The positive reaction was that there's finally somebody here in charge who is going through what we're going through. The negative for some people was, "When are we getting a priest? This is temporary; there's a priest around the corner. He's just here for a short while, then we'll get our real minister in here." Which kind of hurt. Now we're to the point where we've worked through that with the parishioners and now they really do relate to us, because our situation is so similar to theirs.

Wives living in the rectory next to the church had an additional adjustment problem. It was one of them who introduced the problem regarding the lack of role models:

> The hardest thing was the fact that there wasn't a role model. I had no idea how to do this. I didn't know what I was supposed to do, or how I was supposed to be. I just had to play it by ear. I'm still playing it by ear. A lot of times I get too involved. I'm over at the office all the time, and then I'll pull back. I won't go over there for awhile, just keep out of the sphere of what's going on.

Some of the wives pitched in and volunteered their services in the early phase of their husbands' parish work, and then pulled back later on. One of them, who said that she had always volunteered in parish work, even before her husband's new job, explained her strategy:

> I feel that you've got to bloom where you're planted, and you might have to put down roots pretty quick because who knows how long you're going to be there. So we've always kind of jumped right in and done whatever we could. I guess I feel a little bit more responsible because of [my husband's] position for volunteering for things. But now we have a lot more help from other parishioners, so I don't feel guilty about not doing everything. I love song leading and I would do that at any church, so I don't do it because of my husband's job.

Another wife who worked as a team with her husband during the first two years, cut back on parish work in the third year when she accepted a full-time job in the public school. However, she continues to work with him in marriage preparation courses and in visits to the sick. She also describes her "wife" part of his job when she acts as "Miss Hospitality Person," preparing refreshments for various parish meetings, but she carefully explains that these things she does voluntarily because she enjoys doing them.

One woman with two young children started the outreach program for the parish when she first arrived, and was a volunteer teacher in the religious education program. She was very interested in those programs, but when their youngest child was born, her husband said, "You've got to quit volunteering. You almost have to stay in the background more." Some of the parishioners immediately noticed her invisibility and were vocal about it. She described an instance when a parishioner complained about her absence at a parish meeting proclaiming, "She should be here at this meeting. She's the parish director's wife." One of the parishioners responded by asking, "How many meetings do you head up for *your* husband?"

This was one of the many instances described to me when parishioners, male as well as female, came to the defense of the pastor's wife regarding unfair expectations of her role. While many spouses of workers in other institutions and organizations are expected to "show up" occasionally for job-related activities, these are usually seasonal, and the wife's absence is not deserving of censure. One of the bishops remarked, "What does the wife have to do with the medical practice of the physician? Well, not much. She's the loving wife, but she's someplace else."

This experience was an unprecedented one for virtually all of the parishioners. Because of the celibacy rule in the Roman Catholic Church, they had no experience of the parish leader's wife working in the parish with or without monetary compensation, as in other Christian religions. The only extra member of the pastoral team in the parishioners' experience was a priest who, as the assistant pastor with a full-time salary, also lived in the rectory.

Eight of the wives in this study were well acquainted with parishioners' expectations and the parish context, because they had been parishioners long before their husbands were appointed as the pastoral administrator of their parish. Since they were not strangers, we would assume that they needed no extra time to become acquainted with the parishioners. However, in every case their husbands were the first nonpriest heading the parish, so these couples had to deal with expectations about his and their new role in the parish. One of these women, hesitant to enter into this new role, consulted with a priest who was a close friend, and told me that she expressed her "pros and cons" about the job to him:

> One of the cons I felt was that there wasn't any model for me, as a wife of someone like this, because there's no one like him. And I never knew my grandfather who was a Methodist minister, but I grew up in the Methodist model of the minister and wife working totally together. And he [the priest] said, "Well, that's just it, there is no model for you, so they're not going to expect anything from you." And when he said that, I felt like the tension coming out of me. I said, "That's great. You mean I don't have to be at altar society meetings and do all those things?"

One wife offered the following advice to other women who might someday find themselves in her position:

> Don't put on a facade, and don't be something you think other people are expecting. Just be yourself and don't try to live up to others' expectations. Be who it is that you want to be, and don't try to fill a role that you think someone else has a need for.

The Invisibility Factor

The issue of the wife's invisibility in the parish was alluded to in several of the interviews. Sometimes it was the wife who made herself invisible by absenting herself from parish functions. The wives' explanations for absences included: her own time-consuming work outside the parish, her efforts to avoid interfering with her husband's work, her family obligations to her children or aging parents, and her own health problems.

One of the wives explained how she made herself invisible:

> The main thing that I try to do is to stay in the background. I don't know that the bishop was comfortable with my position, and I told him in the beginning that this was [my husband's] appointment and that I was not going to interfere. I wanted him to know that even though I'm involved, the decisions would be made by him, and not by me. And he was comfortable with that.

A wife with a full-time job as a school principal explained why she never put herself in the pastor's wife role:

> I know myself well enough to know that that's an arena that my husband and I cannot function in together in our leadership capacity. See, I'd have the whole crew on Saturday painting that church. I can't stand it. It's filthy dirty. It would be my place, not his place.

It was this same woman who used the term "low profile."

> As far as even voicing opinions, I don't write letters to the parish council. There are things that go on that I may not approve of, but I don't say a whole lot because I don't want to put my husband in a bad position. I just

keep a real low profile. It's like teaching your husband or wife to drive, and it's not my cup of tea. He's got somebody [as a wife] who's not super involved [in the parish] because I like what I'm doing; I've got my career.

The question of turf, or "Who's in control?," emerged when one of the male parishioners who described the involvement of the pastor's wife as "a potentially touchy issue," defended the wife's invisibility:

Now I have a business and my wife doesn't really get involved in the business at all. We do things together all the time, but she really is not involved in the company. As far as the [pastor's] wife being involved in his job, it may create problems for him. You know, he's got his job to do, but then he's also got to watch what his wife is doing because she may offend somebody, and the next thing you know, he's protecting that situation. You know, it could get touchy.

A wife with a full-time job that was very meaningful to her, described her husband's parish as "the other woman in my life," because he consistently worked overtime. However, she emphasized the positive aspects:

He's not involved in my work, and I come home and bounce things off of him because I want somebody to talk to that's not involved in my job. I feel like he needs somebody to do the same, and he'll come home and bounce things off of me.

In some situations the wife was made invisible by others. These situations involved seemingly deliberate acts on the part of others to make her seem invisible by downplaying her presence in the parish. Reasons for the latter were more difficult to pin down, but tended to involve a denial of her presence on the part of those who did not embrace the notion of having a married person as a head of the parish.

Several of the wives spoke about how they were made invisible by the bishop during his first visit to their parish. The bishops in question may have failed to introduce the wife and children out of awkwardness on their part, or because they could not recall their first names. No matter what the motive or intent, not being introduced was a disappointment to the wives.

One wife said that she was both irritated and upset during the installation ceremony when she was sitting in front with her children, because "they never made reference to me or the children." She added,

> I remembered, though, that there's no model for me, and so I shouldn't expect that. In a way, maybe I wanted to have my cake and eat it too. I don't want to do anything in the parish, but I want people to know who I am. But they didn't introduce me, and that kind of bothered me.

Another wife described a situation when the bishop seemed to ignore her presence on his first visit to their parish during a dinner prior to confirmation ceremonies.

> We had been there for four months. Not one question was directed to me about how this was going. I thought that was strange. Maybe it's arrogance on my part. I remember thinking, "I bet he thinks I'm the housekeeper." He let the kids play with his staff and miter, and he was pretty engaged with the kids. But he never referred to my role. Which surprised me, because it is

such a new thing, you'd think he would want to get some information. "Is it going well? Is it going horrible? Do they throw eggs at you every week?" That kind of thing.

Another described a similar experience with a priest sent from the bishop's office to the parish for her husband's installation:

> I had met this man several times before. Not only was my name never even mentioned, or that [my husband] had a family, not only did that not occur during the installation, but the man had to be reintroduced to me when we were downstairs in the reception line. It was like us [the family] being there was so inconsequential.

In other cases it was a parishioner or a group of parishioners who seemed to ignore the presence of the wife and children.

> The people have been very welcoming and have received us well, and for the most part I think that is still true. However there is still a group that, as I'm sitting here contemplating this, I'm thinking, "I'll bet that they tried to deny that the kids and I were here." We were kind of ignored.

Roles for Pastors' Wives

In contrast to those parish situations where the wife was, in effect, invisible, there were other situations where she was often in the spotlight. In these situations her visibility was centered on her activities as a helper to her husband and to the parish, not as a person who trespassed on her husband's turf. The role of these wives could be compared to a first lady like Eleanor Roosevelt, who traveled throughout the country at

President Roosevelt's request, and became the "eyes and ears" for her husband in each place she visited.[2] Such women play very strong, but always supporting roles. Eleanor Roosevelt is often contrasted to the less active first ladies, who spent most of their time in the White House either preparing or serving as hostesses for state occasions, overseeing the work of the staff, and accompanying their husbands on official travels within and outside the country.

One of the parishioners mentioned this comparison when speaking of the wife's influence:

> I think she has a very strong influence, because I think [she and her husband] discuss and share most every aspect of the parish life. I think it's like the president and his wife. You know, the president's wife is not the president, but she has great influence. And I think if you work as a team, a husband-and-wife team, whether you vote or not, you're going to have a great influence.

Only one of the wives in my study was appointed with her husband to head the parish as a team. In the church bulletin she and her husband are listed as the resident pastoral ministers. This was an extraordinary exception, even more so because she and her husband split the work in half, and each received a separate salary check and had separate insurance policies as well.

Some of the pastors' wives overextended themselves in their volunteer parish work. One wife volunteered as parish receptionist and bookkeeper, and also found time to serve on several parish committees. In fact, she was literally working full time for the parish with no financial compensation. In spite of that, she told me that she "never felt she was doing enough." At the end of our interview, however, her words of advice to other women who might one day be moving into the pastor's wife role were: "Don't overextend yourself."

By contrast, one of the younger wives described her negative feelings about her initial involvement in the parish, and about tensions as a result of the fusion of the work and home, prior to beginning her teaching job in a nearby public school:

> The first two years we were working as a team, and we did everything together. We visited the sick together. We did too much together. I was going crazy. We were working together, living together, eating together. I mean it got to the point if we went out to eat together it was like this: "Let's bring a newspaper, we've already talked about everything. Our whole life was together. We were one person instead of two."

One wife estimated that she did volunteer work at the parish at least twenty hours a week and sometimes more because she wanted to support her husband in everything he did. She said that she also did it because he was so busy at the parish that in order to be with him, she had to roll up her sleeves and join him at his job site.

The visiting priest was referring to this same wife when he said,

> She has been extremely loyal to him and supportive. At a cost to her, she's done some leadership things herself. I think it's always a tricky role for the wife of a minister to know how to be one, and there's a whole set of people loyal to her, and a set of people that are not. She's the one who consistently challenges him to take time for his family and for himself. And they've had their struggles around that. But she's not a wimp around him. She really asks for the time, and demands it, and I think rightfully so.

Some of the parishioners used the wife as a sounding board by approaching her with a new idea for her reaction to it, and then asking her to bring it up to her husband. A wife explained, "They realize that they can get to him also through me."

Likewise, other wives alluded to their role as an "antenna," listening and watching for cues that would help to make their husband's performance in the parish more effective. As members of the "audience" at various parish functions, and in casual conversations with other parishioners, they picked up on ideas that would help him to do a better job. This can be a priceless resource for a pastor, particularly in the first few months in his new role.

For example, one wife described the occasion when the priest was unable to make it to the parish on a Sunday. This was the very first time it had ever happened in the parish, and her husband simply announced that they would have a scripture reading and communion service instead of a Mass. The wife, who was present on this occasion, said,

> I could feel the fracas that was going on in back of me in the audience. This particular family [sitting behind me] was very annoyed that this would go on.
>
> And I said to him [later] that I think that a word of explanation ought to have gone on first, like "If there's anybody who wants to leave to go and find another church today," those people would have had a nice out.

Another example of the wife serving as an "antenna" was the role of ghostwriter. Often the husbands would talk over their ideas for the Sunday sermon with their wives. Other husbands would ask their wives to read and edit the written text. In one case, the wife confessed that she sometimes, in effect, wrote the homilies that her husband gave during Mass. She often began by suggesting topics, ideas, and examples from her own daily experiences, reading, and conversations.

[My husband] has a way of taking my thoughts or little stories and putting them into words that are a lot more entertaining than I can. I kind of give him the ideas and then he figures out how to put it into a homily-type form. A lot of times he'll give me his homily, like maybe an hour before Mass, and I'll say that it's not going to work, and he'll change it.

Like Eleanor Roosevelt, these wives served as another set of eyes and ears for their husbands, and also counseled them on occasion. After looking at both the wives' almost invisible as well as highly visible roles in the parish, it is clear that there was no "one way" to be the wife of a Catholic pastor. The wives engaged in a variety of ways to negotiate their roles in a changing situation.

Financial and Health Issues

Both the husbands and their wives tended to place two items high on their list of concerns: financial resources and the physical well-being of family members. One wife told me that before her family moved to the parish, she "spoke straight" to the bishop about the salary they were proposing for her husband. When she laid out the family's needs and responsibilities, the bishop made it financially possible for them to make the move.

The need to supplement the family's financial resources was the chief reason why many of the wives were working full time. In general, they described their work as meaningful, and all but one said that even if their husbands had higher salaries, they would not resign from their jobs. The one exception was a full-time teacher who confessed that her husband loved his work, but she was making a sacrifice for the family's sake by continuing to work:

If my salary wasn't needed, I would stay home. I would do volunteer work, but I don't think I would be teaching because I like it, but I don't love it.

Three of the full-time salaried wives were paid much higher salaries than their husbands, enough so that the family could have survived on the their salary alone. This is an important cushion for these men, who do not have tenure in their parish jobs.

One woman explained,

We could live on what I make. And that was actually a consideration [when he decided to take the job], because he was only appointed in one-year segments. So it puts us in a pretty precarious position every year. But my salary is sufficient for us to live on if we need to. We might not be able to send our daughter to a Catholic high school or to spend $1,000 a month for childcare, and we might have to cut back. But we could never live on what he makes.[3]

This wife was very positive, not only about her own work, but also about her husband's work in the parish. She explained, "To me, it's important that one of us in the house is doing some kind of spiritual work of mercy."

Almost the same sentiments came from another wife with a similar salary:

I have a job that brings us good money. It doesn't offer anything to the world at large. It's not spiritually valuable. My husband does something that is spiritually valuable. He has a far more important job than I do. But my job has secular status. It brings us money. I travel. I have position, authority. But those are not important.

In fact, less than a year after I completed my travels to the parishes, one of the married pastors was informed by the bishop that a priest had been found to take over his parish, and that he was no longer needed. When his wife spoke to me about it on the telephone, she said that she was grateful for her well-paying job, because it could support the family while her husband searched for another position.

A commitment to simple living was mentioned several times during the conversations I had with these couples. For instance, a younger wife who worked with her husband as a part-time director of the religious education program, expressed these values. This was a small and poor rural parish, where the typical family income was near poverty level. When I interviewed her, she had been working as a full-time teacher in the local public school for a year, and she had this to say about financial resources:

> When my husband and I got married we decided to have simple living as part of our marriage, and that we wouldn't be looking for a lot of material gain. And that's probably another thing that has enabled us to do things that aren't necessarily the best economic advantage to us.

The wives who were working in the parish, either for pay or as volunteers, mentioned other rewards. One of the women who logged many hours per week in volunteer service said that two years after their arrival, the bishop addressed their Christmas card to "Mr. and Mrs." She interpreted this as a sign that she was at least acknowledged. To her it was a small, but significant gesture on his part. Another bishop mentioned the wife and children in a letter to the parishioners regarding his appointment as pastoral administrator, a gesture that the family cherished.

When health became an issue for either the wife or the husband, they employed several strategies to alleviate the pain. During a telephone conversation prior to my arrival at the parish, a wife told me that her husband was planning to retire soon, and she added, "I'm burned out." I learned later that her burnout was directly related to her overextended voluntary activities in a parish with a very tight budget. She and her husband lived in the church rectory, where she was the receptionist, bookkeeper, secretary, and housekeeper. She also served on parish outreach committees. Her husband described her as "a compassionate, caring, loving person who gives and gives until there isn't anymore."

> She loved working in the parish and visiting people, but it got too big. At home, she's by herself, and she needs to be around people. The winters, especially, are very difficult for her, with the lack of sun, that whole depression type thing; it's a very complex situation.

His wife, on the other hand, related it to her unrealistic expectations about the parishioners' reactions to her, and she blamed herself.

> I didn't feel appreciated. You know, that's probably my own fault. I can't expect people to have known there was so much to do; yet it would have been nice if somebody had said, "Gee, why don't you let me do the church bulletins?" Or something like that. People didn't offer until it came right down to the wire. And that's my own problem to deal with.

This was not the first time I heard the word "depression." It came up with two other wives who were overextended in parish work. One of these linked her depression to multiple stresses, all of them occurring in the same year: her mother's death, her difficult pregnancy, and the move to the new parish. During this period, without revealing it to the parishioners, her husband took

THE PASTOR'S WIFE ✦ 103

over all the child-care and housekeeping duties, because she was not able to perform them.

This wife talked about a suicidal moment while she was driving the car, and was feeling that everything was on top of her and she couldn't get out from under it. At that moment, she prayed, "Lord, just take me out." She told me that it was her husband who nursed her back to health.

> The only person I could reach out to was my husband, because the hole I was into was so deep. He said, "We're going to get through it, and I'm here for you."

On the other hand, a wife whose cancer was discovered shortly before she and her husband moved to the parish, spoke glowingly of the parishioners' support. She said that they kept bringing things to the parish house, and added,

> They knew when I got here that I couldn't do very much, and we had a supper brought in every night. I couldn't move or anything like that. So to me that was very touching.

She also suggested that her sickness was a positive factor in her husband's acceptance as the first nonpriest to head the parish. She said that the overall acceptance was just wonderful. "I mean, it could have been such a hornet's nest. And it wasn't. They were willing to give us a chance."

The only instance when the husband's health was alluded to was when one of the wives, toward the end of our interview, introduced the topic. She said that her husband was hospitalized for cluster headaches a few years ago, and he was still experiencing them, and sometimes the headaches were so severe that he was unable to drive himself home from work.

The source of his strength is the suffering that goes on inside of him continually, and he will never talk about it. He will never complain about it. That comes from a very deep faith, that he can be so empathetic to the sick and to other people. But I also think that it's a depth of spirituality for him. He is really a suffering servant, suffering in the sense of physical pain.

In addition to prayer and sacrifice, other strategies to alleviate the suffering caused by poor health were mentioned. Two wives left the parish for a time in order to relieve their depression. A pastor's wife said the fact that she was not given any guidance about what she should do in her situation contributed to her depression. She also said, "It's hard to find a support group of women whose husbands are doing the same thing that my husband is doing." One of the parishioners recommended that the wife of a pastor should learn how to say no, and to ask for help when she needs it.

Support Groups: "There Go My Friends"

The strategy that the wives and their husbands tended to use in order to alleviate the pain caused by unclear role expectations, illness, and lack of financial resources was their involvement in a support group. The wives were equally divided between those who were already living in the parish or in one nearby before their husbands were appointed the parish leader, and those who came to the parish from another locale. One wife who had been a parishioner before her husband was appointed to be its leader, described how she lost friends who lived in the parish after his appointment. Many of these friends were upset because they had lost their priest pastor, and were unhappy at the new arrangement. She said, "It changed the relationship with our friends." On reflection she admitted that she had, in fact, anticipated her friends' response. She said that as soon as it became clear that her husband would be wearing an alb and giving homilies, her thinking was, "There go my friends."

The ideal support group needed for this experience should be made up of other women who, like them, were wives of non-priests heading Catholic parishes. As we saw in the chapter 1, such women are few and far between. Consequently many of the women said they had no support group, and those who did have support groups, reported a variety of sources. Some relied on groups that were already operating as support groups for them: a breast cancer group, an alcoholics anonymous group, a prayer group, or (in the case of the deacons' wives) the local deacons' group. One of the deacons' wives said,

> My closest support group would be the wives of the deacons. As parishioners they are more likely to understand because their husbands are active in their deacon work.

A visiting priest said he was convinced that every new structure needs a support group where people can open their hearts and lives to each other. In his view the ideal support group for the new pastor and his wife would consist of similar couples that would support one another. One of the wives described such a couple as their support group: a Protestant minister and his wife about her age who were both ministers at a neighboring church in their town. She reported that she and her husband socialized with them about once a month. In addition she tried to get together with the wife to go for a walk occasionally, "even if it's for twenty minutes," because she had no close friends in her own parish.

Another wife said that she wasted no time in beginning to search for a support group when she moved into the parish. She said that she kept searching until she found one, "Because some-times you just have to sit and talk about your problems."

Views about the Future: "He's Found His Niche"

Given all of the structural constraints, unclear role expecta-tions, health and financial issues, and the paucity of support groups, one would not expect that these wives would view the future through rose-colored glasses. As the data in the appendix show, the dwindling number of priests is the chief reason why the husbands of these women are presently heading a parish. Would these women encourage their children to aspire to the priesthood? The stereotype of the typical Catholic mother as a promoter of vocations to the priesthood, the one who proudly received the first blessing of her son on his ordination day, was prevalent prior to Vatican II and the contemporary women's movement. It lingers on today in parishes throughout the country.

Because mothers are still viewed as the parent chiefly responsible for the children's socialization, their current view of the future of parish life is crucial. When they spoke about the priesthood, the women whom I interviewed tended to be ambiva-lent. However, one of them expressed a strong negative view when she said that she would not want her husband or her sons to be priests. As she explained it, "It's too exclusive. It's unjust. The exclusion is sinful and it brings people excruciating pain."

The wives who were positive about the future referred to their husbands' jobs as a "calling." One of the wives explained,

> I'm proud of him and all that's happening here. I think he's found his niche, and it's good for him. He's grown a lot, doing this. He really feels a calling. What you want for your husband is to be happily employed at what he's supposed to be doing, and this is probably the

first time that he has had that opportunity. So it's been good for him, and in turn it's good for the family.

All the married men in my study, both lay and clergy, know that their future as parish leaders resides in the hands of their local bishop. They also know that sometimes a new bishop's arrival can trigger a firing of nonpriests heading parishes. In fact this happened to one of the married leaders less than a year after our interview. When I was visiting their parish, his wife expressed her feelings about her husband's pastoral work this way, not knowing at that time that it was a prophetic statement:

> I have found it a very spiritual path for me, marrying somebody who has a calling to serve God and the Church in this capacity. My husband will always be working for or with the Church in some way, shape, or form. So this is just a chapter, which may be a long chapter or a short chapter. It depends on the changes in the Church.

When the wife of a lay leader began to speak about the future, she reminded me that both her husband and she worked full time, and they have a growing family that needs their time and attention. She then concluded,

> So it's challenging. I think when he's done we'll both look at each other and just be exhausted. But I also think that we've benefited. It's been a very growing experience for us. If he doesn't do it for the rest of his life, that's okay with me. If he does do it for the rest of his life, I believe we can make the right decision about it.

Even though they had neither role models nor support groups made up of wives of pastoral administrators, these wives, with the help of their spouses and the parishioners, managed to create a number of strategies that helped them to expand the options for other women whose husbands are newly appointed as parish leaders.

Summary

In his study of the wives of ten priests who converted to Catholicism, Joseph Fichter found that their husbands were helping out in parishes by saying Mass on the weekends, and though they did not live in the rectory, and in most cases did not live within the parish boundaries, they were "generally available for infant baptisms, confessions, funerals, wakes, weddings, and sick calls."[4] All of the priests in Fichter's study had a full-time salaried job outside the parish, whereas that was true of only three of the men in my study. Only half of the women in my study, those who were married to deacons, are wives of Catholic clergy. On the other hand, all of them are wives of men heading Catholic parishes, an experience that, according to the guidelines of the American Bishops, is denied to convert priests and to former Catholic priests who are married.

In many ways the wives in this study are breaking new ground. None of them is the wife of a priest, but they are married to men who have been appointed by the bishop to be the leaders of Catholic parishes in dioceses throughout the United States. Their presence belies the argument that married men cannot successfully administer Roman Catholic parishes. The current statistics on the priest shortage in the United States found in the appendix shows that the category with the largest number of non-priests entrusted to head parishes are laypeople. Though religious sisters are the second largest group to head parishes, their numbers are dwindling, so we can expect that the numbers of parishes headed by laity will continue to increase.[5]

Because they have no role models, these wives are creating different ways of being a pastor's wife, in many cases recasting their position by showing that it is not necessary for wives to give up their own meaningful occupation outside the home when their husband accepts the appointment. Like other women pioneering in new roles, this has not been a smooth process for them and their families. Nonetheless, these wives occupy a key position in a changing situation that is gaining some momentum in the United States: Roman Catholic parishes administered by married men.

Chapter 4

The Pastor's Children: "But I'm Only a Kid!"

I conducted interviews with the pastor's children in only thirteen of the twenty parishes. Two of the pastoral administrators were childless, and the children of five parish leaders were either too young to be interviewed, or they were older, and either away at college or living out of town with their own families when I interviewed their parents. The average age of the pastors' children was twenty-one years old at that time.

On the first parish visit, I was concerned that the children might "freeze" during the interview, so I decided to incorporate some "getting acquainted time" before I broached the subject of the interview with them. The three children had met me on the first day of my visit when I took the family out to dinner and encountered me on other occasions at the church and in their home, the former rectory. I also asked their father if I could accompany him when he drove his oldest son to a local school for a Saturday class on driver education, so that I could try my hand at drawing the boy out. This turned out to be a disaster, in my view, because all I could educe from the boy were polite but terse responses.

When I described that scene to the mother, she invited me to their home for supper on the day before my departure, the same day we had planned for her interview. She also suggested that I take the three children out for ice cream right after supper before mentioning their interview.

Her strategy worked beautifully. The children and I had a great time eating our ice cream, and choosing the ice cream for their parents. In fact, we were "pals" by the time we returned home. When I finally broached the subject of the interview to them at their home, the youngest was the first to react. He asked, "Will we be able to talk into the tape recorder like Mom did?" Once the three of them learned that they would be treated like the grown-ups, they were eager to begin their group interview. After about five minutes of taping, I interrupted to rewind the tape so they could hear how they sounded. It worked like magic! All three were enthusiastic interviewees.

The issues that emerged from group interviews with the children in these parishes included: moving to a new location, the rectory as "home," the role of a Catholic "pastor's kid," kids as parishioners, having your dad as the pastor, kids who were "deviant," and kids at work.

Moving to a New Location

I asked the parents how they prepared the children for making a geographical move. For some, it was an unexpected change, and there was little time for their children to get used to the idea. For others, there was time to adjust, because the move was not imminent. As one of the pastoral administrators explained, both he and his wife talked to their children about it, but did not ask their permission. They kept telling them, "This is what it looks like, and we might be going there."

When I interviewed the children, two big concerns regarding the move emerged: changing schools and losing friends, but they also mentioned some advantages of moving to a new location.

Two of the three children of a layman heading a rural parish said they didn't mind their father taking the new job, but they were reluctant to move from their present location in a city because all of their friends were there. The third said that he felt the same way, but "after I thought about it for a little while, I thought it would be interesting to be somewhere new, and have new people around."

The youngest said he found the move difficult because he preferred his former school. He admitted that he "doesn't hate it here," but wished that he were back in the other school. Later his father told me that his children's former school was a parochial school, and it provided not only an excellent education, but it was also "a warm, friendly place, so it was difficult for them to come here."

This family was situated in a small town where they were attending the closest public school. The daughter declared,

> There's just one thing that I don't like about living out here. It's really nice, but there aren't a lot of people to meet; there's not a lot of people to make friends with. So, like, I only have like two friends.

She also said that she really loved being an altar server, but her brothers were sometimes teased and called "the church boys" in a derogatory way by other kids at their school. Her older brother dismissed this behavior by saying, "Well, that's only the people who are dumb, and nobody really likes to hang out with them anyway." And he added, "We've learned to live with that sort of stuff."

On the other hand, the daughter of a deacon in a parish on the outskirts of a large city said that when they moved to his parish, she was excited that her father had a job that was "more stable," and she found the parishioners "real friendly, like a little community." She added,

> And you know, my dad was in charge, so it was like we had little privileges, like they'd say, "Oh, you're the Deacon's kids." So it was nice, and the house and everything was exciting.

Another father was already a member of the parish, and had worked as a deacon there for several years prior to his appointment as the parish leader. His married daughter, who traveled from another town for the interview, described her initial reaction to the news of his appointment:

I was excited, because he had decided to get out of the family business and go out on his own. And this would give him a steady income. So I thought he probably knew more about the parish and the people because he had worked with them. And you know, I think he's been there fifteen or sixteen years now.

A daughter expressed her feelings about the move.

I was a little scared, because we had really close friends right next to us. I was really scared, but I was still kind of excited, too. I didn't know much about small town life, and about what it would be like to have my dad run the majority of the church duties. So I just didn't know what to expect.

Another daughter described the bishop's participation at her father's installation:

I remember he was making jokes about my dad, but everybody does. He was just teasing him. But it was neat to hear the bishop say good things about my dad, too. That he felt comfortable giving my dad this position, and things like that. That kind of made me feel a little bit better. It was good, and it was neat. It was weird as far as saying to my friends [who invited me to play with them that day], "Oh, no…that day I have my

dad's installation." It's different. You can't explain it to
people very easily.

The son of a lay leader in a rural parish gave this testimony:

When we first moved here, people were very hos-
pitable. There was a boy who lived down the road, and
he must have been about fifteen or so, and I was ten. It
must have been heck for him to come over and hang
out with a little kid, but he did, just so I could get used
to the first year of being here.

The Rectory as "Home"

The living arrangements of the families varied: (1) Five of
the twenty families had moved into the rectory shortly after the
father's appointment. Three of these parish leaders were deacons
and two were laymen. (2) Five families, who had been members
of the parish for a number of years before the father's appointment, chose to remain living in their own homes. (3) Five families who lived outside the parish boundaries remained in their
own homes because the father's parish was close enough for him
to commute to work. (4) The remaining five families, who lived
a considerable distance from the church, moved from their previous homes, and bought or rented a house near to the church.
Even those fifteen families living in their own homes, however,
shared an experience similar to that of the five families living in
rectories: the need to separate their family space from their
father's work space.

During the interviews I asked each person about the advantages and disadvantages of the parish leader's family living (or not
living) in the parish house. All of them expressed their views about
the living arrangements, but the children residing in rectories

were so eager to speak on this issue that I placed the discussion of the housing situation here. One of these, a twelve-year-old boy whose family was living in the rectory just a few yards from the church, whom I will call "Bobby,"[1] said:

> Because we live near a church, everyone expects us to be so perfect. I know that you don't need to be perfect because nobody really is perfect. So most of the people [in the parish] have come to know me as somebody who is just normal.

Bobby told me about an incident that happened soon after they moved into the rectory. As he was walking out of the door of the rectory one day, Bobby tripped on a stair, and said, "Shit!" An older woman who was walking down the outside stairs of the church heard what he said and admonished him, saying, "You shouldn't use words like that. You're living in a holy place." To which he replied, "But I'm only a kid."

When Bobby described this incident to me, there was no sign of embarrassment, and he said he did not feel it was necessary for him to apologize. In his view, what this parishioner needed to understand was that the situation had changed. No longer was a "holy person," like a priest or a sister, living in the rectory. Bobby was attempting to keep this parishioner from invading his family space, where he felt free to be not perfect, but normal.

Although living in the rectory meant larger quarters for these families, there were other problematic features. One of these complaints was voiced by a teenaged daughter, who mentioned her embarrassment the first time a potential "date" discovered that she lived in a church rectory. Although her date did not back down, she felt her "church home" was a deterrent for future dates.

For an understanding of another family member's views on rectory living, here is a vignette from one of my interviews with "Ann," the wife of a parish leader.

Ann, the wife of Deacon John, is seated on a couch in the parlor of the rectory, where her family has lived since her husband was appointed to head St. Mary's Catholic Church. While nervously twisting her fingers, Ann tells me that this house has never really felt like "home" to her. In fact, she said it was like "living in a glass house."

Ann explains that the parlor we are occupying and the adjoining dining room are used for parish committee meetings and religious education classes, because the church has neither a basement nor a parish hall. She then points to a table at the other end of the parlor where a small group of parishioners gathers on Wednesdays during the winter to attend word and communion services. The family's kitchen on the first floor is also used for snacks and coffee while these parish activities are going on. With a sigh Ann adds that their private space on the second floor is often invaded when the noises from the evening meetings carry to their bedrooms and the children complain that they can't sleep.

Ann's oldest daughter, a parent herself by the time of her interview, elaborated on the family's situation when she said,

> My mother felt invaded, completely invaded. And there wasn't anything to do about it. She had to have her dishes done when people came for these meetings at 7:00 or people were going to see that she didn't have her dishes done. You know, there was still this notion, "your house is a reflection of you."

Ann's avoidance of embarrassment and her daughter's observations suggest that there is more to this situation. When she elaborated on the invasion of living space, Ann's image of the glass house seemed even more formidable. Ann admitted that she feels some of her house is, in fact, "off limits" for her. She said that she hesitates walking downstairs in her bathrobe to use her own kitchen for fear of running into a parishioner. With a touch of anger in her voice, Ann admitted that she was often dismayed the next morning when she went down to fix breakfast and found the sink filled with dirty dishes.

What she was describing was the penetration of workspace into family space.[2] That the family's living area became a parish working area was attested to by Ann's daughter, who told me, "Even though the meetings were supposed to be in the dining room, it didn't keep anyone from going anywhere in the house."

Ann was angry and depressed about her situation, but she also was struggling to resign herself to the invasion of the family space, for the sake of her husband, who loved his job. One of the male parishioners told me that both Ann and her husband "felt that this [their home] was parish property and everybody should have access to it, and they did." He concluded, "It's a big strain on a couple to live that way."

This strain resulted in Ann's decision to move out of the parish house and stay with relatives for an extended period of time. When she returned, the family members were not able to create enough space where they could all relax and be themselves. Ultimately this situation led to her husband's decision to take early retirement and move the family to another part of the country.

Priests and bishops also mentioned the stress they experienced living in rectories. One referred to it negatively as "living above the store," another as "living in a goldfish bowl." One bishop used the latter term when he said,

> We have a policy in place that says a priest may move out of a rectory. We have a growing number of rectories that are empty because the priest has said, "This has become increasingly a parish center."

He continued,

And I live in one of those parishes. [For instance], if I am in my jeans and I'm making supper for myself, after a meeting there are people who come in [to the kitchen] and say, "Excuse me, I just want to use the coffee pot. It impinges on one's sense of having a little space where you're not on duty...the goldfish bowl.

Another bishop said,

My preference would be that they [married men and their families] not necessarily live right where the rectory is. I don't like the idea of having their bedroom right over the office....I'd like people to begin to see the difference between them serving as a minister and being who they are called to be as family, also. I'm struggling with our priests along the same lines, especially the priests who live in one-man rectories.

Another vignette illustrates the strategies, feelings, and perceptions of those who were more successful at establishing a better arrangement.

Deacon Andrew and his wife Betty live in a rectory that is only a few feet away from St. Mary's Church and the adjoining parish offices and classrooms. Their grown-up children do not reside in the rectory with their parents. The rectory, a one-story brick building, is located in a small farming town five miles from the main highway. Deacon Andrew is enthusiastic about his living situation:

I love it. I love being able to run back and forth at a whim. When I forget something or need to copy something, I can just [snapping his fingers] do it. I can just run over here [to his office] and do it. I just figure I'm on tap. I've always kind of been that way. I don't think it bothers [his wife] any. The only times it's a little bit annoying is phone calls.

His wife, however, had no intention of living in a rectory indefinitely. Her reluctance to make the move from her family home two hours away was assuaged by her daughter's willingness to move back to the family home and "keep the home fires burning." Nonetheless, Betty had strong feelings about her new living space, and saw to it that the secretary's office was moved out of the rectory before they arrived. "When we moved down here, I said, 'Now this rectory is going to be our home. It's not going to be a rectory while we're here.'"

Deacon Andrew and Betty used a strategy that. was quite common in the families I visited. In order to separate home from workspace, they had two telephone lines installed. In many cases the home number of the pastor's family was unlisted. But some like Deacon Andrew were ambivalent.

> Nobody in this parish has that second number. It doesn't ring over here [in the parish office] any more. But Betty gets mad at me [when I answer the church number at home]. She says, Why don't you just let it go? You're off. Don't worry about it." But I'm kind of compulsive. I always answer the phone.

The Role of a Catholic "Pastor's Kid": "People Watching Me"

Two issues the children raised about their role as a Catholic "pastor's kid" were the way the people scrutinized their actions inside and outside the parish and what they liked and disliked about their own participation as members of their dad's parish.

Several of the children mentioned that they felt some parishioners and others in the town placed them under close scrutiny because of their fathers' position. One of the boys, whose father was the leader of a parish in a suburban area said,

> When me and my friends go out, there's always somebody who knows me from the church who will just watch me, so I can't do anything wrong.

A daughter described her experiences as similar to the children of the "first family." She then elaborated,

> I know everybody watches me. I mean, when we're in church, it's like we're THE family. I know that. And I think, even when I took my boyfriend to church, "everybody's watching." Maybe it's more in my head than it's actually happening. So maybe I'm just more aware of that.

Another child who felt "watched," said,

> But there's lots of gossip about a church man and his family in small towns because they're looking for someone to be perfect, or they're looking for someone who they think shouldn't ever screw up, and when they do, it's just over, it's all over.

A daughter talked about walking around in a grocery store in a small town, where "people from the parish are just eagle eyes....You're always being watched."

One of the sons also inferred that sometimes people reported his actions to his parents:

> One of my friends was trying to set me up with a girl, and my mom walks up to me one day and says, "Oh, so

and so is trying to set you up with her, huh?" And it's like, "Oh, geez!"

Another son complained,

Some people think, like at church, we have to be all goody-goody and act all sweet, and I don't like that. Sometimes we can't be ourselves. We have to be extra, extra polite.

It was a deacon's daughter who made the following recommendations:

Just be yourself. Realize that as soon as you take on the role of the deacon's daughter, people's perceptions about you change. You're no longer just the kid in church. You're the deacon's daughter or son. They kind of like put you on a pedestal and they expect you to act in a certain way. My brother, he's a rebel and he's not supposed to wear shorts in church, but he'll do it anyway.

Another daughter said that she felt that others had different expectations for her because of her father's position. For instance, when she arrived at a party with her high school friends, people would remark, "You're here?" She described her reaction in this way:

And it's like, "Yes, I'm here. Everybody else is here, too." They kind of assumed that I must be, you know, almost above the rest.

One of the wives shared some important insights regarding her children's experiences.

I think they noticed it when [my husband] was given the assignment, that they became the favored children. It was like the children of the first family. Actually our kids have always been involved in the parish, but the expectations were unrealistic sometimes. When [my daughter and her boyfriend] would go out and people would see them, we would hear about it the next day at church. They would be angry, and say, "We just want to be like everybody else!"

The wife concluded, "Sometimes the expectations are unrealistic because all pastors' children are treated differently, and much more is expected of them. It's stressful for them."

By contrast, the children of a deacon in a poor rural area said they did not experience trouble from the other kids. One of the sons said,

No trouble at all. Around here, being a preacher or pastor is pretty normal because there's a lot of churches. We even go to school with some boys who are preacher's kids. So there's a couple of my classmates who are preacher's kids themselves, so then it doesn't seem too weird for your dad to be a preacher if your classmates are also, you know.

Kids as Parishioners

Some of the children of these parish leaders were more active as parishioners than others, so their experiences varied in both quantity and quality. For instance, a mother reported that her teenaged daughter served as a sacristan in the parish, and another daughter and son were altar servers. A daughter in another parish described her participation:

Ever since we've been at this parish, I've been serving, setting up the tables for church dinners, help cook food and chop vegetables. I help out because [my father's] like part of the church.

A son reported why he had cut back on church attendance:

I've been to church ever since I was born. And I've been at the church 100 percent, and know the ceremonies by heart. And once I started to get older and jobs started coming, I cut back a little bit. And now my dad's real open. He tells us to go to church, but says, "You're a grown adult now. You decide." He's one of the most understanding dads ever.

His brother agreed with this assessment:

He never pushed us. I mean, he left it up to us, and he still does. Like he won't say anything. The only thing he'll tell us is, "It'd be nice to see you in church. It'd be nice if you could make it." And you know, he doesn't push it, because everybody's different, and he understands that.

Another issue regarding church attendance was the placement of the parish leaders' family members during the Sunday Mass. One of the daughters remarked that the "little things mean a lot" and then mentioned a family strategy:

I just happened to think about seating in church. Like my mom and my family, we don't sit like in the first pew. We kind of sit like in the middle of the church, so we can be with the people. So they don't think, "Oh, since they're the deacon's family, they have to sit in the front of the church."

And another thing my mom pays close attention to is when we enter and leave the church. Because it kind of looks bad if we show up late, you know."

The children also discussed the problem regarding the physical separation from their father when they attended Mass in their parish church. They were seated in the main body with the other parishioners, while their father was on the altar with the priest and altar servers. One child frowned when he said, "We can't sit with him at church." Another son voiced his complaint:

Like for Easter or for Christmas that we want to do as a family, it's been hard, and we've had to adjust to it. We understand his job, but at the same time, you know, we'd like to have him down with us.

His younger sister added, "I would miss him a lot and want him to sit with me. But because he was always so busy, he couldn't." Sometimes the parish leader would mention his children when he was delivering the Sunday homily. One of the children commented, "Sometimes it's kind of weird if he's talking about something that you did or something." But she assured me that her use of the word "weird" meant "just strange." Her brother agreed, and testified that his father would seldom use their names, but instead say "my son," or "my daughter," but most of the parishioners knew to whom he was referring. The older daughter explained, "It doesn't make me sad or anything." And her sister said, "It's kind of neat to hear him say that, though."

A parish leader described his three children as "very involved" in the parish. He said that both of his older children help with the liturgy and serve as Sunday school teachers. His daughter volunteered to be the main accompanist for the choir, and his son occasionally served as a song leader and as a lector during Mass. Even the youngest helped out by setting the table for coffee and doughnuts after Mass.

Their other activities during Mass mentioned by the children included ushering, taking up the collection, bringing the bread and wine up to the altar during the offertory, and singing in the choir. There was only one case, mentioned earlier, where the family members were not active parishioners in the married leader's church, because they were still living at home in their former parish where their mother was a full-time teacher in the parish school. The son explained the extent of the family's participation in his father's new parish:

> We've gone to Mass there a few times. We went there for Christmas Mass. They had an outdoor Mass over the summer that we went to. And those bigger occasions, we'll go as a family.

There was another parish I visited where the wife was actively involved, but not her teenaged children. The visiting priest assessed it this way, "Maybe the kids haven't adjusted to this area. Maybe they didn't want to come here. I don't know what the problem is."

While I was meeting with a representative group of parishioners in each parish, one of the items we discussed was the issue of vocations to the priesthood. The young men in these groups typically showed no interest, but one of them did say that he was interested in becoming a priest. In spite of that, he said that he would not be applying to a seminary as a candidate because he highly valued family life and wanted to have a wife and children of his own.

Even children who were faithful churchgoers talked about why they had no interest in following in their father's footsteps. When we discussed the priesthood, a younger daughter, whose family lived in the church rectory, said that she would not want to be a priest, and she felt that "it would be kind of weird." Her brother agreed:

> You would spend a lot of time sitting in the office and stuff. You'd be taking calls, and when you got off the phone, it would ring again. And then you'd have to go out to every church meeting.

The older daughter in this same family gave the children in her family a new title: "Well, we've been around it so much. It's kind of like we've been 'kid-priests.' That's what it seems like."

Her younger sister, however, had the last word on the topic. She laughed as she remarked, "Now if we were ALL priests, it'd be kind of neat."

A prospective candidate for parish leadership emerged when I was interviewing the wife of a deacon who had two sons and a daughter. This wife stated that her two sons were involved in the church when they were young and growing up, but now they think that it's "too much work." On the other hand, she described her daughter as "very reflective" and "often volunteers to be an altar server." In fact she quoted her daughter's words, "I want to be a deacon just like dad."

Having Your Dad as the Pastor

Equating "dad" and "pastor" suggests a tension between home and church. And so it was for the children of these Roman Catholic parish leaders. For them, there were no role models to look to for guidance. Their closest mentors would be children of Protestant pastors, with a long tradition of married pastors. But most of them were newcomers when they arrived at their present location, and even at the time of their interview, some had not yet met other "pastors' kids." Thus it was difficult for them to deal with dad's long absences from the family and to assess his various duties in this new job.

A teenaged son began by describing his father as "totally, always at church," but he quickly added, "Not always, but he's there a lot. He's been at church a lot lately, because we're building a new church. He's been gone a lot, so we don't get to spend as much time with him."

By contrast, a younger daughter noted an increase of her father's presence at home over time. She explained,

> He used to not even come back home until we were in bed. He used to come back really late because he would be doing a whole bunch of stuff for the church. And now he comes home for dinner, and oftentimes he comes home for lunch, so it's good that way.

A wife, whose family was not prepared for their father's long absences, described her dilemma in this way:

> It was hard. You know, "Where's Dad?" "He's at a meeting." "Where's Dad?" "In another meeting." And so it really got to them as they were growing up, because he doesn't have all that time to spend with them.

A son gave this advice to future children of pastoral administrators: "Expect to not be spending as much time with your father, because he'll be doing more stuff at the church. And expect to be doing more things for the church, and be more involved."

In spite of the drawbacks associated with the issue of their father's time away from home, family members expressed their willingness to support him in this new endeavor. A daughter said,

He's really happy with it, so I think that's kind of taken care of some of the stress. I haven't been hearing so many negative things from my mother. So I'm assuming she's changed, too. It's different now, in a good way.

There was a change over time with regard to the children's experiences and attitudes about their father's duties in the parish. One of the sons described it this way:

As far as him being in charge of services and things like that, at first it made me feel uncomfortable. And it was like, "I can't believe he's doing this." Embarrassment, you know. But I was young at the time as well, and since then I've kind of got over it. I realize he has to be himself up there, as well as being a pastor. So I'm not embarrassed about it any more.

His sister added,

At first I thought how it was that, you know, he's not a priest and he's doing almost all the same things that a priest does. And when we have a visitor passing through town at our services, if they introduce themselves to me after church, I say, "He's my dad!" And they look at me like, "What? He's your DAD?"

The children also expressed great pride in their dad's accomplishments as the leader of the parish. One of them described the previous priest pastor as an "older gentleman who was set in his old-fashioned ways," and then said,

The church was growing, and they needed somebody to go in there and take control of it. From what I hear, there were financial problems at the church. My dad has totally turned that around. My dad's a people person. He gets along with anybody, and he loves to help people. So, you know, when he got that job, I was really happy for him. And I still am.

Another daughter said that she was "really excited for her father," when he was appointed to his new position, because "this was something he wanted to do." With great pride, she said, "Daddy is the priest for the church."

A son said he was "comfortable with it, but seeing him on the altar is kind of weird." Nonetheless, he concluded by saying, "He's very happy with what he's doing, and he's really gotten into it. He's totally jumped into it with both feet. So I'm happy that he's happy."

A deacon's wife told me that she felt "very blessed" about her husband's role in the parish. As she expressed it, "Every problem that we've had, it turns out to be a blessing." But she admitted that her husband's new role had a different meaning for her son in his relationship to the parishioners. She said, "The only thing he does say is that they look at him like he can do no wrong. He feels that he has to put up a front, because he's the son."

One of the high points for these men was their family's assessment of his role on the occasions when he participated in church services for members of the immediate family. One of the daughters described an unforgettable experience for the family, her father's eulogy at his own mother's funeral:

> It was fabulous. Everybody was so very proud of him. My grandmother is from a very large family, and I think her sisters were hesitant about my dad doing it, because there were several priests presiding also. But it was just a true blessing to everybody.

A deacon's daughter said,

My dad married me and my husband. It was very, very special. The church was something my grandfather had helped start in this little community, and my father was up at the altar. The whole thing was so significant, and so beautiful.

Another deacon's daughter recalled a memorable occasion:

I can remember being at my parents' house one week-end when the son of somebody in the parish committed suicide, and the police came to the house to get my father to bring him to the family. I guess that was one of my first-hand experiences of watching him minister to someone in the parish. It was a major crisis. That only serves to reinforce how capable I thought he was of doing well by other people.

One of the deacons, who was close to retirement, talked about some of the high points of his career:

I married both of my girls, and I baptized two of my grandchildren. That was something special. A lot of the weddings I've performed were for former students, their family and friends. Those were all high points.

Kids Who Were "Deviant"

As might be expected, not all of the children were conform-ists. Although they tended to be proud of their father's new position in the church, there were limits to the degree to which they wanted to be active parishioners and to meet the expectations regarding the typical "pastor's kids" role. Unlike the Protestant "pastor's kids," there were no role models for them in Catholic parishes. These children were, in fact, creating a new role. In that sense they were like their father, a married nonpriest pastor in a Catholic parish. Two "deviance" issues that emerged in the interviews were attendance at church services and conforming to expectations about premarital sex and sexual orientation.

An example of a "deviant" offspring was a high school-aged son who said that he was rebelling, not only about going to church, but he was really questioning religion in general. His parents did not force their son to go to Mass every Sunday, but they did require him to go on Christmas, Thanksgiving, and Easter, so they could celebrate these events as a family. The daughter, a college student, did not resent this, but the son did. Their father told me that it was very hard to sit back and see his son in this rebellious stage, and it would be a comfort to him if his son were active in the church. However, he stated that once he reaches eighteen, he will no longer be required to attend Mass with the family on special occasions.

The son expressed his thoughts and feelings about his situation:

> One of the biggest things is how other people perceive you. I mean, "son of a preacher man." It's just kind of a contrast. My dad's religious, he's read the Bible, knows every word, went to the seminary for a couple of years. And I agree with nothing of that. Generally you'd expect somebody who has their dad be practically a priest…you'd expect their kids to be fairly religious.

This "deviant son" also pointed out that his father's job was "not the highest paying job, and he works long hours for not a lot a lot of money." But he concluded by stating, "The nice thing is that you're going to meet interesting people. And all of his friends are always nice to me."

The deacon in a Native American village voiced his concern about the lack of participation of younger parishioners: "Most of the young people don't come anymore, even my kids. That's the main thing we're worrying about."

I found that the sons of parish leaders who lived in the parish rectory tended to resist the presumption that they were not only eager to sign up as altar servers themselves, but because of their proximity to the church, they were also willing to substitute for the acolytes who failed to show up. One "deviant" altar server said he preferred to stay home and "do stuff that I want to do" rather than serve on the altar in his father's parish. He proclaimed, "I really do not like serving, standing up that long. The robes are hot. I don't like it at all." Another younger son told me that he really liked serving, but he let the other servers know that he would not fill in as a substitute for them.

A teenaged daughter who often served as accompanist during the hymns at Mass, discussed her ambivalence about her role:

> It was a big step for me to volunteer to play every Sunday at church. And I don't think I would have if Dad hadn't been the pastor. But I think that if he wasn't the pastor now, I still probably would, because I do enjoy doing it. Although it gets old sometimes, knowing that I have to go. I would rather once in awhile just go to church, not to be there because they need me to play.

One of the pastor's sons, whose fiancée was pregnant prior to the marriage, confessed that they waited to inform his father until they felt comfortable enough to approach him with the news. He continued,

> But my dad expects so much from us that when we told him, it hurt him. Because when he goes to church and he's up there on the altar, and he's talking about premarital sex, he's talking about the way the Catholic Church believes. You know, it's just like a double standard. That's

one thing we apologize for, but we're the ones who did it. A lot of people don't like to listen to him or take him too seriously because of what we have done. And a lot of people understand that our mistakes are something that we did, not what he did. And that's something that he has to deal with every day.

He then described his father's reaction to the news:

My dad was a little upset. But you couldn't ask for more supportive parents. He said, "You made a mistake. You're human. But your Mom and I support you one hundred percent."

A married leader told me that his daughter was eight months pregnant when she graduated from high school, and that this experience helped him to "deal with a lot of other families who have gone through that situation." He added, "I made a lot of mistakes that a lot of people don't know anything about. She made a mistake and it was very obvious because she couldn't hide it."

Another parish leader told me that his daughter, who was married by him in the parish church, was now separated from her husband. Her father described the occasion when this daughter came to tell her parents that she was a lesbian:

It was difficult for her to tell us. She's a good mother. And I can't dislike [her partner]. She's a nice person, and she's a good person. We've had friends of ours say "Well, we wouldn't let them in our house." It was difficult for us, but until you walk in somebody's shoes....She's still our daughter. And it makes me more tolerant of differences.

Her father reflected on his own reactions to the news:

It was so devastating at first. I mean of all people, I
would never in my wildest dreams...[My daughter] is
very, very much like me, in so many ways. On the
Myers-Briggs personality profile—we've both taken
it—we're identical. We're so much alike, but I don't
really understand the lesbian lifestyle.

While her father was concluding the discussion about his
daughter, he shed some tears. Although he talked about how he
has learned to accept it, it was not easy for him to express his feelings. But he made it clear that he treasures his relationship with
his daughter, and that he will not prohibit her partner from coming with her on her visits to his house.

Their daughter gave an account of her parents' reactions
during our interview when she was discussing the issue of "people
looking at you and making judgments." She said, "I think there's
an added burden of your children's lives and your children's per-
fections and transgressions. I know that my being gay has been a
real struggle for mom in the church."

A lay parish leader spoke of his family's experience of other
forms of deviance, like teenagers with drinking problems. He said
that parents would come to him, and "seem to feel pretty comfortable that I've probably been through some of this, and know
what they're talking about." He also suggested that he is probably
"bringing another dimension" to the marriage preparation course
in the parish.

Kids at Work: "Helping Dad Out"

Although the younger children depended on their parents
for their economic needs, several of the older ones made a financial

contribution to the family. A high school graduate described his work schedule. He said it began in the morning, when he helped out on his grandparents' farm until noon, and then, after eating his main meal, he went to his full-time job in town, from 2:30 until 11 P.M. When I asked him if he also helped his mother to take care of the grandparents, he laughed and said, "Yeah. They're a full-time job."

Another son who had finished high school and was living at home was also working at two full-time jobs. His daytime job was at the local airport, and he worked a night shift at another location as well. Altogether he calculated that he only had about five or six hours of sleep per night during the week.

Like other young people throughout the country, some of these sons and daughters had part-time jobs such as baby-sitting, clerking at stores, cutting grass, shoveling snow, and doing other odd jobs for the neighbors. One of the wives described her children's contributions: "All my kids paid part of their tuition. They would work during the summer, and they would have to pay a certain amount toward their tuition."

A lay parish leader, whose wife was a full-time teacher in a Catholic grade school, said that both his teenaged son at home, and his daughter away at college had part-time jobs. He explained that his daughter had a scholarship that covered about one-sixth of the total cost, and then said, "Our son's saving up for college. He knows that he's not going to get into the kind of school he wants to with our salaries."

Another way of "helping dad out" for the kids at home was to take responsibility for chores around the house and yard. One of the older sons presented some advice to future "pastor's kids." He said,

> Be supportive, basically, because it's a big responsibility. Do a lot, help your dad out, basically. Don't argue with him, because he's going to have a stressful job. If he's

stressed and agitated, he needs some time alone. You have to understand this, so just be a little lighter on him because he's tired.

Several of the children spoke about "helping dad out" by volunteer work at the parish, like folding and stapling church bulletins, serving during Mass as lector or acolyte, answering phones, and helping out with church dinners. One of the sons had a suggestion for other kids who wanted to help their father: volunteering to set up the church for big occasions, like Christmas or Easter.

His younger brother, on the other hand, had a piece of advice for future pastors' kids that illustrated the tension between two communities: family and parish. He strongly suggested that they avoid something that really "bugged him": waiting for his parents after Mass on Sunday when he was anxious to get home. His advice was,

> Get your parents out of church as soon as possible, because they'll just sit around and talk for hours. Everybody wants to sit around and talk to him. So bug them, take them by the collar and just drag them.

Another "pastor's kid" gave this advice: "Get involved with helping around the church. Sometimes it's fun, like at the festivals. It's kind of fun, and you get to know people."

One of the sons, who volunteered to be an acolyte at his father's church, laughed when he said that he continued to volunteer "until I outgrew the cassock." He then explained his motivation:

> I wanted to be up there [on the altar] because I wanted to do it, not because someone's forcing me to do it. But at the same time, I felt, "Gosh, this would sure be a great help to Dad." A lot of times I would do it just week after week after week because there was just

nobody else to do it. And now there are girl servers, and there's probably a little more surplus now of servers.

One of the teenaged daughters said that she was glad that she volunteered to help out at the parish two days a week for a couple of weeks in the summer, as a substitute for a woman in the front office who was on vacation. She said she volunteered because she was interested in learning more about the context of her dad's new job. She said,

> I was just answering phones and keeping up the records. People were very friendly. I wanted to kind of see what the situation was. And after my mom heard that I was doing it, that's when she decided that she wanted to, so she was there for about a week and a half.

An older son described how his father opened a new opportunity for him when he invited him to come with him on visits to the elderly "shut-ins" of the parish. He said,

> I've been to several elderly people's homes. And I've seen him give communion to them. I've even established relationships with the people he's giving communion to. Some of them have died, but I still have that memory of them.

One of the assisting priests pointed to another way that children help their father by their presence: when a family moves to a parish in an entirely new part of the country, especially during the first few weeks in the new parish. He said, "I think the family is really helpful for the support issue. And if they've got children, it's an immediate entry into the community."

An older son described how he helped his father to prepare a sermon for an unusual audience. He explained that he was a teenager at the time, and that he "hung around" with a lot of different people, some of whom were members of local gangs, and a lot of gang members were expected to be present for this funeral for one of their members. He said that when his father approached him about this,

> He asked me, basically, the right words to say, so they wouldn't be offended. It was kind of touchy. He asked me about the different things to say, like "How does this sound?" Afterwards, gang members came up to me and said, "Your dad really put a strong message across." And everybody was like, "Wow!" Because people were going into church in their gang shirts, you know. And my dad put it straight up. If he had used the wrong words, people would have been mad.

Summary

The children of the parish leaders are well aware of the adjustments related to the role of a "pastor's kid." Nonetheless, they tended to be positive about their experiences in the parish, and proud of their fathers' new role. In fact, teenaged sons spoke of their new status as an advantage in a dating situation, because of the good reputation of a parish leader. The younger children who were outgoing and loquacious sometimes functioned as "ice breakers" for parishioners who were awkward about conversing with their new leader and his family, especially in the first few weeks of their arrival.

On the downside, moving to a new location meant the loss of friends and close scrutiny for these children. The close scrutiny was especially difficult for children in the five families living in the rectory. However, there were two additional benefits for these families. Living in the rectory meant free housing, more space for the family members, and a short walk to work for the father. The children in the five families who had been members of the parish previous to their father's new position had the dual advantage of continuity in their living arrangements and in parish membership.

Not only did seventeen of the mothers work for pay outside the home, but the children themselves also tended to contribute to the financial support of the family by taking part-time jobs. The experiences of these families call into question the argument that Catholic parishes cannot afford to hire married pastors because the resources of other members of the family, children as well as wives, have been overlooked.

Chapter 5
Parishioners:
Community Building

Although the married leaders and their families, the priests, and the bishops have important roles to play in these parishes, it is the parishioners who will continue to be the mainstay of the parish, well after some of the other central players either move away or die. In my meetings with a representative group of parishioners in each of the twenty parishes, the following issues emerged: the meaning and mission of parishes, strategies for community building, location and size of parishes, closing parishes, outreach to the larger community, ownership and participation, and parish liturgies and other celebrations

The Meaning and Mission of a Parish

A married leader in a large but poor parish located in the inner city spoke about the dual mission of the members of a parish: creating a community of faith in the parish itself and establishing outreach programs to meet the needs of people outside the parish community. He compared the dual functions of the parish to a flower that is "opening and closing."

> It has to be, first of all, a praying community. It has to be bound in the word of God and Eucharist. And then there's the outreach to the community. It's like one of those flowers that opens and closes. So it brings together, and then blossoms. That would be the image I would use.

When parishioners spoke of their definitions of a parish, the words "family" or "community" were mentioned over and over again. One of the parish leaders who grew up in a large Italian family whose family reunions included over a hundred people said this:

> I think parish is a faith community, and I use the model that I know, which is my family. This big family shared goals and dreams and backgrounds, but also a lot of differences, and unique skills that they bring to the group.

A parishioner in a Mexican American parish described his parish as "very family active:"

> This parish has been like a large family from way back, generations and generations. That encourages me to get my kids here, because his [the pastor's] kids are here. His kids go to high school with my kids. It makes it more family inclined than just the church you go to every Sunday. I'm willing to do just about anything he asks me to.

One of the deacons described the difficulties he faced regarding his decision to accept the bishop's appointment to head the parish. He had a full-time job outside the parish, and his parish was situated in a poor urban area on the edge of the central city. It had been merged with two other parishes that were closed shortly before he arrived as its pastor. He told me that he first consulted all of the principal characters in his life, and after much prayer, he made the decision.

> I accepted because I think that's what God was calling me to do. I thought what the church would look like and would be like under a different structure, that it

should be more of a "family–type" structure versus someone really being over the parish rather than working with it. And I said, "Wow!" This was a perfect opportunity for a parish of this type to really blossom and find itself.

Another parish leader spoke of the need for parishioners to identify who they are and where they're going, and he quoted from a mission statement that was the result of two years of input from his parishioners:

The first line says, "We are a mosaic community." Because we realize that we have all the way from the traditionalists to the conservatives to the liberals here. And color and culture, too. So they came up with the word "mosaic." And every piece counts.

A parish leader in a predominantly Hispanic parish said,

I think the parish should be a place where people can come together, share their life experiences, and be available to the needs of others. The parish should be a safe place where people can come and don't feel intimidated by a lot of bureaucracy, a place where they can come and worship, come to know Jesus Christ, not only through the sacraments, but through each other. It's like the family, a place that offers them services. So a parish has to be life giving, and it has to be one of service.

A parishioner in another Hispanic parish who described himself as "heavily involved" in the parish, referred to it as his "second home." He added, "I don't mind the time I put in, because I understand my call from God. It's a way of helping my brothers and sisters here." Another woman in the same parish who was serving a six-year term on the parish council, said, " It's a lot of work, especially when I have small kids at home." Nonetheless, she concluded that the parish gave her a "sense of belonging."

A parishioner said this about her parish:

> Being single, this is kind of like my family here. I mean I am totally immersed in this place. It's like a big part of my life, in every aspect. I mean, my family is here, because I'm from another city, and don't have a lot of blood family.

Her fellow parishioner added,

> The parish community has always been very open and accepting, like right now there's a very large gay and lesbian part of the community. If it weren't for this church, they'd probably be associated with no Catholic church.

By contrast, in one parish with a noncollaborative leader, a parishioner attested to the lack of a communal bond:

> I have to say that never once in the seven years we've been coming here, felt like at one, jelled with this entire parish. There have been individual times when I felt a group of us come together and really jelled. But I've never felt the entire parish come together for one big occasion.

One of the priests described a parish in a small rural town where he saw the parish as the "hub, the center of everyone's life, Protestants as well as Catholics." He explained that the local Protestant minister sent his teenagers to the priest when they got in trouble, "because he didn't know how to handle them." In the poor inner city parish where he was now serving as the sacramental minister, the priest gave the example of a white family who lost their house in a fire, and "an African American parishioner who owned a house near the church, gave this family his house for a year without rent." The priest concluded,

> That's what a parish should be. It's not the buildings. It's not the school. It's none of that. I think the parish is a group of worshiping people that are supportive of one another in the good times and bad.

A parish leader in a small parish in the deep South presented his definition: "The parish is a community of faith that is grounded in the local community, a community that takes the Gospel seriously, and sees all people as God's children and all people as brothers and sisters."

An assisting priest said that a parish "ought to be a Eucharistic community where we gather at the Eucharist and draw strength from the Eucharist." He added,

> I think the Eucharist is a tremendous bonding experi-
> ence, or it should be. I think it's done off handed a lot
> of times by priests who are maybe burnt out or what-
> ever. That's why even when I feel tired, I try to con-
> centrate on the idea that you must feel this, and you
> must communicate the significance of what's happening
> here. And that's very hard sometimes, but at the same
> time, it's the peak moment.

Strategies for Building a Parish Community

An assisting priest described the part the married leader played in the formation of the parish community:

I think the way he formed the community is by sharing the vision with them and letting them express the vision. He is like one who holds the canvas and lets them come up and paint. And I think it's a common project they're working on. They're looking out together to see the things that need to be done.

An African American deacon said this about his parishioners:

I'm ministering to a people who over the years just came to church on Sunday, received communion, and went back home. So the whole process of finance, administration, religious education, all the components that make up a church, the African American community over the last fifteen years has not been involved on that level of the church. So you have to build that. And part of the building is helping people to understand why we do what we do, how the church functions, and why it's important to have religious education and stewardship. When you start to do that, the level of involvement is very low, because you're dealing with a mindset of "All I'm supposed to do is come to church on Sundays, get communion, and say my prayers."

A bishop described a strategy for community building that was used in one of the parishes I visited, situated in a small community a long distance from any city or large suburban area:

[The parish leader] has developed a communal sharing list in the parish. People with anything at all to share in the parish are listed, including their talents, and directories are distributed to all parishioners. It gets people to know one another.

When I visited this parish, the parishioners were eager to describe how the "sharing list" worked. For instance, one of the parishioners said,

> If I need a punch bowl and I don't have one, or I need a paper typed and I can't type, or I need someone to cultivate my garden, and this person has a cultivator, they'll bring it up and do it.

They also explained that someone who needed to borrow a sewing machine could reciprocate by contributing hours of baby-sitting, or someone who needed time on another person's computer could trade by helping that person to mow the lawn or to rake leaves. In short, the parishioners applauded their pastor's idea of a sharing list, because it increased their resources and strengthened their relationships.

Another strategy for building a parish community was "work days." A married leader described it this way:

> In the fall, a group of men and women come. Some work inside to clean the pews in the church or paint windows, and some climb up on the building to do the tuck pointing. We announce it so that everybody knows it's happening, and then we start calling people to make sure some people will be there.

Parish dances for various age groups were mentioned many times. Other gatherings where relationships were deepened included parish picnics on the parish grounds and Sunday breakfasts in the parish hall.

One of the parishioners mentioned camping out as a means for social cohesion:

The word goes out that we have this many campsites, and who wants to come, and we spend the whole weekend together. We have a sense of family that's unspoken. There's a feeling that this parish has provided for me and [my wife] that we've never felt before: just a real part of belonging and being able to call on any of these people in a time of need. I could pick up the phone and say, "We're really hurting here. We need some help." Or, "We want to share this with you." To me, that's community.

I heard a farewell sermon delivered by a parish leader in which he echoed the Vatican II definition of the church as the "people of God." On the eve of his departure, he reminded his parishioners that they are the Church, that their hands are the hands of Christ and that their feet are the feet of Christ. The parishioners received his message with a hushed silence, but they broke into applause at the end of Mass as he walked down the aisle of the church.

A parishioner spoke of the spiritual growth she experienced in the parish:

It's been a place for me of great spiritual growth. I find myself thinking, "Well, four or five years ago I would not have thought of myself being involved in things that I am today." And I feel so much better because of it now.

Location and Size of Parishes

There were some differences between both rural and urban and large and small parishes. The rural parishes and the inner-city parishes tended to have fewer resources than the urban parishes. One of the Hispanic deacons described the neighborhood where his church was located as a barrio. Driving into the neighborhood, one can see that the houses are small and old, but neatly kept up.

Most homes had flowers growing in the front yard, but the cars parked on the streets were typically old and battered. As the deacon described it,

> You go to a ritzy church or an Anglo church, and there have been new buildings built, and so forth. The barrio church, unfortunately, was created for the purpose of segregation, and keeping the classes separate.

A white deacon in charge of a predominantly African American parish, told me that the church was located in a poor and "dangerous neighborhood." Nonetheless, he drives into the neighborhood every day of the week except Saturday to visit the homebound parishioners. The deacon also told me that the parish building had been broken into many times, so they hired a caretaker, who lives on the third floor of the building with his family. When I arrived at the church parking lot on Sunday, the security guard directed me to a parking place, and announced, "Your car will be secure."

One of the parishioners in a small African American parish talked about the difference between small and large churches:

> In the huge churches, people shy away from their feelings. But you come here, and you can let your feelings get away and exposed, because you have other people sitting here doing the same thing. You're somewhat bashful in a larger church because you're going to have so many staring eyes at you when you try to express yourself.

A parish leader in a small rural parish described the dedication ceremony for the new church, where every parishioner in that small community played an important part, like singing in the choir or carrying items up to the altar (the baptismal bowl, the keys to the church, and the financial plan). And he concluded by saying, "So we really kind of tried to get people to see that it wasn't the bishop and me and my wife, and say to them, 'See, this is the community.'"

A bishop referred to size of community when he was describing the parish where he had appointed a Hispanic deacon who had been a member of the predominantly Hispanic parish before he was appointed the leader:

> He has a great love for that community, and they know that. Again, there's a bondedness that goes back over a number of years. He's had a relationship with his people. He knows them like the back of his hand, and they know him. It's a small community, a confined community, within a certain geographical area.

A lay parish leader in a small community said that sometimes, in a teasing manner, he refers to his parish as "the cathedral." And when the bishop heard him say this, he asked, "Why do you call it the cathedral?" His reply to the bishop was, "Well, how many times have you ever heard of a bishop closing the cathedral?"

This parish leader discussed the issues of size and location with me:

> That's always a fear in a rural parish, and not just this one. That definition of viability and vitality is related to size, and I say, "Let's look at the faith community. Let's look at that dimension, knowing it's hard to measure. But let's use that as a reason, instead of saying, 'Well, let's have big parishes.'"

He also described a component part of a faith community as "lots of caring people." And he related it to the size of a parish when he described a recent episode in his parish. One Sunday, just as people were arriving at the church for Mass, the rescue squad arrived across the street from the church, at the home of an older female member of the parish. He continued,

> Nobody could pray, because right across the street, they had the rescue squad for her. Finally [a family member] got word to the priest, and he interrupted the whole Mass and said, "She's okay, and she's at the hospital now." I mean, nobody could think of anything but Mrs....Why doesn't that happen in larger places? It's unfortunate that those are the places that get closed.

A bishop addressed the issue of parish closings:

> We would not close a parish simply on the basis of limited available priest personnel. We're trying to recognize the validity of a parish community as a faith community. Some of our parish communities, some of them originally ethnic parishes, have become more weekend shrines than parish communities. People feel an allegiance to be registered members, but only come for Mass on the weekend, and the end result is you don't have the full faith community. We've had parishes that have had no baptisms for three years.
>
> So we've looked for indicators of a faith community, and we have found ourselves saying, "Look, a viable faith community includes weekend worship, it includes education, it includes some community activities, and some outreach to the poor." We're trying to help people understand that a viable parish community has to have a certain amount of resources, fiscal and human, in order to do the mission. We have also said we would not close a viable parish community, even

though it was small, if we know that it is in an area that is growing.

Outreach to the Larger Community

One of the parishioners in a small rural area reported that her parish leader was involved in an interdenominational community, and he had taken an active part as a preacher at interdenominational revivals. She also said that he had made several visits to the hospital to see her Methodist father, who was suffering from Alzheimer's disease. "And he would bring a little portable radio, and play old hymns that Dad grew up with."

At another geographic location, where the "church" was a rented storefront building, parishioners reported that their parish leader had been elected the vice president of a local ecumenical group that included Methodists and Presbyterians. When I spoke to the parish leader, he described his association with a local Baptist church whose pastor was head of the Baptist Association.

> The pastor of the First Baptist Church has been real supportive. He invited me to preach in his church at their Thanksgiving service. And I got a hate letter from one of the Baptist pastors from an independent Baptist church that's not aligned with the Baptist Association, saying that I was an agent of the pope who wants to take over the world, and put everybody under the rule of Rome.
>
> And [the Baptist pastor] was real apologetic about that happening, and said that there is still a lot of ignorance around here. And he said he was really sorry it happened, and that I shouldn't get too worked up about it.

The parishioners in a rural parish reported the following ecumenical outreach projects: (1) Services together with all of the churches in that town at Thanksgiving. (2) An ecumenical service four times a year, one of which includes joining together for a Good Friday walk, carrying the cross to every church. (3) An ecumenical bible school for young people from all of the churches. The visiting priest for this parish said that he admired the married leader for his effectiveness in creating a bridge to other ecumenical groups in the community, and the priest admitted that it was something he doesn't do very well himself.

The parish leader in another small town described the formation of an emergency coalition now called the Extra Mile Ministry. Six months after he arrived in the town, there was a tornado, and this is his account:

> Quite a few homes were wrecked, and people were left without a place to live. We did some calling around to see how we could help out, and there just wasn't an apparatus for churches to work together. There wasn't a Red Cross. So we started something called the Emergency Coalition, where we invited people from the churches and community agencies to get together to talk about how we can work together better. We published a resource manual on what services were available, and we're working with the social service agencies to see if we can't learn some skills on helping people find jobs and other things.

One of the parish leaders described a program called Food Service, formed by the churches and social agencies of his town. He described it as a "cooperative buying sort of thing," and said,

> They buy a whole truckload of groceries and people pay a smaller amount for it. We had to have a minimum

of 60 orders to sign up. We had 360 sign up, and 700 people were waiting at the Methodist church when the truck was late the first time. People were crowding the doors, and waiting in line, when someone suggested, "Let's get everyone to sit down in the church." So we did. And that was the most people I've ever seen in any church here.

We started singing, and I sort of took the leadership role. We asked, "Are there any pianists or organists in the crowd?" We kind of had an informal worship experience. People sang a bunch of songs and hymns, and we opened up for spontaneous prayer, and people just shared. And I told people, "This is the largest congregation in our county."

Outreach programs also operated in parishes located in the inner city. One of the parishes I visited had a neighborhood center that was initially established to care for the neighborhood's elderly or mentally disabled residents. It also offered two other services: adult day care so that family caregivers have some needed respite, and a kids' café where neighborhood children have hot meals. Another group of parishioners in an inner-city parish was working with the Bread for the World movement to help feed the hungry.

Ownership and Participation:
A "Beehive of Activity"

The parishioners in these parishes without resident priests tended to be actively involved, because they were fearful that their parish might be closed. A bishop explained,

In that parish, they had been told that their parish would probably be closed and this might be their last pastor. This deacon could have been King Kong and they would have accepted him! They were so afraid that their parish was going to be closed that they were open to whatever was going to happen, because they wanted their parish to be open.

It was during an interview with another bishop that I heard the phrase "beehive of activity." The bishop was describing the transformation that he had witnessed at a parish headed by a deacon. He described the church offices and meeting rooms on the lower floor of the church that were once seldom used, as now teeming with activity from early morning until late at night. The laity of that parish had, in essence, "taken over" those spaces for committee meetings, classes, prayer services, and other activities.

In fact, I witnessed that phenomenon myself when I arrived at a church parking lot on a Sunday morning at 8:00 for the 8:15 Mass, and observed that the lot was already almost full. The place was bustling with people helping to prepare the church for Mass, and the downstairs classrooms for religion instruction that took place immediately after the Mass. In fact, several of the offices were already open and occupied.

The factors conducive to this parish community building mentioned most often by my interviewees were: transmitting a sense of ownership to the parishioners, the need for participation in their own parish activities, and establishing a welcoming atmosphere for parishioners and others outside the parish.

A deacon used the image of church as home when he said,

When I look at the church itself, I look at a house, a home. I look at the people that operate in the church, that come to the church feeling that this is their home, to feel responsible for all that really takes place in a home, having people pick up and take care of their responsibilities.

I asked this deacon how he discovered the talents of his people after he was assigned to this parish.

> I try to be with our people, every opportunity, chatting with a person who's out cutting the grass or working in the kitchen. You learn what people's interests, skills, talents are. I just see myself as a family member. If there's a function where we're serving a meal, I pull up a chair and try to make sure I'm not sitting with the same person all the time, that I learn who people are.

A young adult parishioner stated,

> I purposely chose this parish. The reason I chose it is because of the family-like atmosphere. The people are warm and welcoming, and the leadership is that of empowerment. There are tensions in any parish atmosphere, but the chance to be the person you are and offer your gifts is more readily accepted in this parish.

The wife of a lay leader told of a "core group" that existed in the parish when her husband was appointed. She described the group as "cliquish."

> He has broadened that core group in a way that has really strengthened the parish and broadened the sense of community. People who were previously afraid to take a leadership position needed to be encouraged, and he sought them out, and tapped them to broaden the core group. So it's no longer the sense of, "Well, everything's being done by the same people."

An African American deacon explained why he had not yet emphasized the need for ecumenical outreach to other churches:

I think it's very important for our church family to know who they are first. I think the whole Catholic Church, the white Church, has imparted to African American Catholics their mindset of "All I'm supposed to do is to come to church on Sunday, get communion, and say my prayers."

He continued,

I find myself having to undo some of that, so we feel good about ourselves and we know who we are. Because there's still some folks yet who are not only not comfortable with being called black, they're not comfortable with being called African American. So there's a lot of education to do there.

When I was in a church one Sunday, seated next to a partially blind African American parishioner, I noticed that the other parishioners were solicitous as they would carefully hand her the missal opened to the proper page at the beginning of Mass, and give her the hymnal with the page opened for each hymn. She would hold each book close, almost touching her nose, and then read the prayers and sing the hymns along with the congregation. At the end of Mass there was applause throughout the church when she stood up and thanked the parishioners who brought her to church.

One of the parishioners described how he and his wife were greeted the first time they attended Mass at the parish church:

We sat someplace in the middle of the church, and when we came out, a woman came up and hugged both my wife and me, and said, "Hi, my name is so and so. Who are you? I've never seen you here before." And we told her who we were, and she said, "Well, we certainly welcome you to our parish, and we hope that you'll come back again."

He continued, "And that's never happened in any church, even in the ones we were very active in. And that sold us."

Another parishioner described a follow-up strategy:

When we became members and filled out our registra-tion form, we had someone call us and come to visit us. Nothing was ever pushed on us. It was just, "Welcome. What can we do to help you? This is what we have available." It was wonderful. And we've come almost every week since then.

Another woman described how she became acquainted with her parishioners after Mass on Sundays:

You go and have coffee and doughnuts afterwards and there's someone ready to talk to you, whether you know them or not. There's always someone talking to you.

Her fellow parishioner added, "I feel that I always have a place to turn, no matter what difficulty my wife or I would encounter."

A parishioner related her leader's marital status to the grow-ing sense of community in the parish:

I think that [my parish leader] having a wife and family, it only added, because it gave the people of the com-munity more of a sense of community, because he was just like everybody else, and had the same situation as everyone else.

A married leader said,

The experience that I bring into the church is the experience that I bring being a member of my own family at home. I cannot function as a father being a dictatorial father. It doesn't work. Listening, being present, admitting that I don't know it all and that sometimes I'm wrong: These things are important. They're the things that take place in my family: seeking forgiveness from family members, allowing one to test the waters, letting go of the reins, and allowing people to fail. Without taking risks, there's no growth there.

He continued,

Someone who doesn't come from a family, that doesn't experience family can't relate to some of this. So when I get in the pulpit on Sunday morning, I try to bring these kinds of stories with me that touch the hearts of people and experience on a day to day basis the same kinds of things. And that when we stand together on Sunday morning, we can hold hands and we can praise God, because we know that it was us holding hands together that brought us through the week to Sunday morning.

A lay pastoral administrator emphasized how he fit the profile of his parish members:

I have the perspective of the people in the pews, because I've been in the pews. My experience with a lot of leaders of faith communities is they've always been on the other side of the communion rail, and they have very little feeling for the people in the pews. I'm a lot like the people themselves. I'm a fairly normal person, and in a somewhat normal marriage with kids. And the big advantage is that I can relate to a lot of what's going on among the people, because the majority of people have been married and have had kids.

When I asked a Mexican American parish leader what his parish meant to him personally, he replied,

> It's really my lifeblood. I love the place. I love the people. I really get a burst of energy serving God's people and being in the church. There's something unique about administering here. When I go and visit people who are homebound or in the hospital, I always come away with a lot more than I walked in with. Those types of situations are the things that really give me the energy and the spirit to keep going.

A female parishioner described her parish in this way: "As I'm getting older, I come closer with some of them than I have with some of my own family members. My social life is my church family."

One group of parishioners took turns describing a practice that strengthens communal ties. One of them explained that on certain occasions, when praying for a parishioner who is extremely ill, or for someone moving away, "The entire community raises their hand, and while putting their hand out, says a prayer, and it brings the whole church together."

Another parishioner described that moment. He said it was "like the flames are shooting from our fingertips within this entire church. It's the greatest sense of community…everyone has their hand up, from the feeble person who can't really get it up, so somebody has to stand there and put it just breast high. But the entire community is together.

An older parishioner described an ecumenical parish practice:

At Christmas time we had a group of 50 or 60 people who walked around the neighborhood singing Christmas carols. We either wind up here or around the corner at the United Methodist Church afterwards and have hot chocolate, coffee, and cookies, demonstrating that the Protestants, the Catholics, and whoever else is out there can all be involved. And I really think that's important to our community.

One of his fellow parishioners followed up with this statement:

It shows a lot more responsibility, doesn't it? I mean you have to be much more responsible for your spiritual community. You can't let the priest carry it for you.

A married leader, who was new to his parish situated in a poor inner-city neighborhood, talked about some strategies to increase a spirit of community:

I see a lot of work to be done. We have ushers and hospitality ministers or greeters, as they're called. So it's through the greeters that we try to really welcome people. Do we do enough of that? No, because we don't do enough follow-up or outreach to building community.

I'd like to eliminate about half the pews in the church. I think that would bring people up a little closer, in terms of physical community. We've lost some community-building activities, like a festival. It's hard to do in this neighborhood. A lot of the other fund-raising or community-type things are often associated with the parish school and younger families. So the older families feel left out. Every second Sunday, though, we have a Holy Name breakfast, and they invite everybody, and the elderly come, and that's kind of nice.

A parishioner in a small Southern parish said,

> You don't feel closed or left out here. You do not hear
> somebody saying, "That person is not good enough.
> He doesn't have enough to meet my standards." I know,
> because I went to quite a few churches here, believe me.
> There would be people who wouldn't look at you. They
> wouldn't like what you had on, they wouldn't like your
> hair, or the way you trimmed your mustache. You don't
> feel closed or left out here.

His fellow parishioner added, "When people come here they
realize that we don't care what you wear. In a lot of churches, you
have to be really dressed to a T, and that's what [he] is trying to say."

Another parishioner in a large city said this about her parish
leader:

> He has a concern and commitment to the group. And
> we come to him like a pastor, like a normal pastor. He's
> like a father figure. There's a connectedness that you
> feel with him.

A bishop summed up the strengths and weaknesses of the
outreach efforts in his diocese in these words:

> Every single parish has a strong commitment to devel-
> oping a religious education program. Every single
> parish has made a real effort to do a better job in liturgy
> and liturgical participation and so forth. We don't have
> the same commitment to social justice, to peace, to
> ecology, to social outreach. That's the ministry we're
> poorest at.

Parish Liturgies and Other Celebrations

The topic of parish liturgies and other celebrations raises two issues: (1) the tension between the importance of community and sacramental values in the celebration of the weekend liturgy, and (2) the inclusion of cultural elements in liturgical celebrations and other gatherings that promote communal bonds.

The issue of "priestless Sundays" and the circumstances under which "word and communion services" can be conducted in a parish will be discussed in the next chapter. A bishop related these services to the value of community:

> Jesus is present in the community gathered, and he is present in the Word proclaimed. So that's two out of three. But a bishop fired a woman who was the pastoral administrator of a parish partly because when there wasn't a priest, instead of encouraging the people to go to another parish for Mass, she did a word and communion service. So that bishop's main idea is if you don't have a priest, send them somewhere else to Mass. So [for him] the Mass is more important than the community. And if there's no priest, that community shouldn't gather. They should go someplace else.

He continued,

> Another way to frame the question is to stress viable faith communities, the full ecclesial community model. "Don't go to communion services" was clearly stressing the sacramental aspect. My sense is that the church has to have a community identity and a base.

Another bishop stated that even though the Eucharist requires the presence of a priest, there are other sacraments. His view is that as long as there are people around to take care of some of the sacraments, it's better than nothing, and it keeps the community together. And he argued that where there is a community, we should encourage that community to stay together. Consequently, he has resolved not to close any parishes, and he will find people to come in and do as much as they can.

How have parishioners reacted to the sacramental limitations of their parish leaders? One of the parishioners in an African American parish led by a deacon who was the prototype of a charismatic leader, said this about his sermons:

> Sometimes when you leave the church, you're about ten pounds lighter [laughs]. And that's no tale. You get a good feeling out of church, but like people say, "You've got to put in, in order to get out." If you sit there and listen to what he says, and it penetrates your body, when you leave the church, you're about ten pounds lighter.

Another parishioner added, "It's just like nourishment. Like you're hungry, and you're fed. You know, 'Hey, I know how to deal with this one now.'"

When a bishop described the training workshops for native ministry programs, he said that it included a program on the spirituality of tribal groups. This was part of the attempt to counter the thrust of earlier evangelization programs.

A Native American deacon who was the parish leader said this about native rites:

> Christianity plays a very important role in doing away with a lot of [our] rites. They outlawed [our] rites and made the old people believe that these are the work of the devil. We have encouragement from the bishops now, and most of the prayers and the homily are in [our

language] now. They used to do it in Latin, and we never knew what was happening.

On the first day of my arrival at this Native American village, I walked over to the church to attend an evening communion service that was scheduled immediately after the recitation of the rosary. When I opened the door, I saw that there were six older people in the church, five women and one man, reciting the rosary in their native tongue. The only word I could understand was "Mary." Unlike the parish leader quoted above, I knew what was happening, but like his marginal position during Latin Masses, I was also unable to participate with these parishioners when they were reciting the prayers in their language. While I was sitting in the back of the small church, waiting for the deacon to arrive for the communion service, I admired their solid wooden church built by the parishioners themselves, and beautifully decorated with colorful tribal ornaments.

Although I expected him to appear on the altar when the rosary was finished, there was no sign of the deacon, and the parishioners were leaving the church. As I followed them down the steps of the church, an older woman smiled at me, so I introduced myself, and asked about the deacon's absence. She said that she heard the deacon had been detained on a visit to another village to assist at a funeral, and would not return until the next day. She then introduced herself, explained that she had been a widow for three years, and welcomed me to her village. She quickly followed it up by inviting me to come with her to her home for tea. There I met her daughter and grandson, who were visiting her, and after they told me the history of their village, her daughter insisted that I return for supper.

This woman was a key figure during my stay in the village. She was the one who informed me that there would be a tribal dance in the village meeting place to honor visitors to the village, and she accompanied me to that ceremony. Mostly young people performed the dances, and the older men, including the deacon, participated by beating the drums and singing. Watching that ceremony helped me to understand the importance of the deacon's dual role as elder of the tribe and leader of the parish. And I was deeply touched when the parishioner who befriended me pronounced her special tribal name in her tribal language, meaning "someone to lean on," and then announced, "I'm going to give you my [tribal] name." Her daughter wrote it out for me and made sure that I could pronounce it correctly, and she also provided access to information for me when she served as my translator for the interview session with the parishioners.

In a Mexican American parish, the deacon described how his parishioners celebrated the feast of Our Lady of Guadalupe. He said that they begin with Mass at 5:30 A.M., followed by Mexican breads and chocolate for breakfast. In the afternoon, starting at 4:45 they have Mexican dances in the social hall, and then a neighborhood procession, followed by a solemn Mass at 6 P.M. that is broadcast on the local radio. The main celebrant at this Mass is usually the bishop, but the deacon and assisting priest are also on the altar. Finally, after Mass they have a big feast day dinner and entertainment by Mexican dancers. In this parish, immigrants are assisted with the paperwork for their documentation, and English as a Second Language courses are also provided for them.

During a Mass at a small rural parish, the wife of the parish leader, who was in charge of the music, turned on a taped hymn during the communion that was sung in Spanish. She told me later that she always does this for the Hispanics in the congregation. There were four Hispanic families among the forty people in the small chapel on the Sunday when I visited the parish.

An assisting priest in a predominantly African American parish spoke of the enrichment he had experienced.

On a personal level, it's a very enriching community for me. It's my first experience in an African American community, and it's just been a wonderful, wonderful experience. It keeps opening my appreciation, my vision of church, and of spirituality. They challenge me to broaden my understanding about church, and about culture. It's so different from what we are as white people, and it's so enriching.

Another example of the inclusion of cultural connections occurred during a Mass in a small parish in the deep South that values informal contact with people in the local schools, stores, and other organizations. Here the first fifteen minutes of the worship service is reserved for a guest from the area who talks about the local community and its activities. This guest is invited to remain for the liturgy and for coffee and refreshments afterward.

My experience at a word and communion service led by a Native American deacon is another illustration of cultural connections. The parishioners not only sang the hymns in their own language, but they also heard it spoken throughout the service. At the end of the service, three or four people stood, and in their tribal tongue gave a message to their people. I was told later that one of the speakers was telling the young people how happy he was to see so many of them, and he thanked them for coming. His words of thanks to the young people did not surprise me, because several parishioners told me earlier that they were worried that the young people were going to lose their tribal traditions, and they were making efforts to strengthen their cultural bonds.

Concluding Statements

I conclude this chapter with two statements about parish life: One from a bishop who made it a practice to visit all of the parishes in his diocese and one from a group of parishioners. The bishop said,

> I see that there is a renewal going on in the church at all levels, and I don't think that that renewal and reform is going to be turned back. I think it's the movement of the Spirit. Liturgy is being renewed, and as I go from parish to parish in this diocese, I see they're really doing a nice job on liturgies. There's participation. People are making real efforts with the environment, with the music, with getting young people involved. Then you have the involvement of people in parish councils, finance councils. People want to be part of the active ministry in the church. That's happening all over the place. There's no way you can say, "Well, you can't be involved in ministry unless I give you permission." That's the way it used to be.

A group of parishioners offered the following definitions of parish:

> A community of believers coming together, working together…
> A place where we get nurtured, feel a part of…
> We share a vision, play and pray and cry together…
> As a community we *become* community, we don't *join* community.

Summary

The parishioners were not ambivalent about the future of their parish because they saw it as an extension of their own families. In fact they tended to be actively engaged in various efforts to build their parish community, making use of such strategies as "sharing lists" and "work days." It was one of the bishops who described a parish with extensive lay participation as a "beehive of activity."

The parishioners themselves testified that they were donating not only more hours, but also more money to their parish since the arrival of their new married leader, because as one parishioner explained proudly, "He's one of us!" Both my observations while visiting these parishes, and my interview sessions with the parishioners, priests, and parish leaders and their families have convinced me that these parishioners are seriously engaged in building community and taking ownership of their parishes.

Chapter 6
Priests as Sacramental Ministers: "Uncharted Territory"

This chapter attempts to shed some light on how the priests who have been placed in an entirely new role make sense of their new situation. These priests who travel to the parishes administered by nonpriests to celebrate Mass and administer other sacraments are given a variety of titles by the diocesan authorities. In thirteen of the parishes I visited, the title was sacramental minister, and in two, it was assisting priest. The titles used in the remaining five parishes were parish chaplain, canonical pastor, visiting priest, pastoral life director, and sacramental priest.

What does this new role mean for these priests, who do not reside in the parish, yet have the responsibility for the sacramental life of that parish? How do these sacramental ministers translate their mandate into action? What strategies do they use to exercise pastoral care in a collaborative way with the married man in charge of that parish?

The subtitle of this chapter comes from a lay parish leader who described how he and his assisting priest worked out their roles on sacramental occasions:

> Weddings, Father and I do it together, and I wear the alb. We're together with that. Funerals, I wear the alb. So part of the paradigm shift is, "What do we do here? This is uncharted territory."

Because the visiting priest is the one with the title "pastor" in this situation, how did his role partners—the married man entrusted with the pastoral care of the parish, the parishioners, and the bishop who appointed him—interact with him in the exercise of his duties. What kinds of strategies did they use to support or hinder various aspects of this evolving role? This chapter attempts to answer these questions with regard to the following issues: ritual leadership and priestly identity, sources of strain and support, and visions for the future.

Liturgical Roles and Priestly Identity

For many priests, the core of his identity is at the altar where he performs his sacramental roles. In these parishes, it is the priest, not the married leader, who presides at the Eucharist on Sunday. One of the priests in my study explained it this way:

> I'm very Eucharistically oriented, to tell you the truth. It has been kind of the center of my life. Sometimes it's the only thing I do every day that makes any sense at all. So it's always a deep moment for me. That's what I'm about. It's the only thing I do that's unique. Anyone can do all the other stuff I do: counseling, run to the hospital, and that kind of stuff. But to preside at the Eucharist is the only thing that the church really is calling me to do.

This conviction about the priestly vocation was echoed by one of the lay leaders of a parish:

> I don't really feel like it's possible for a nonordained person to be pastor. To me, the pastor really is the spiritual leader of a community. I think the main gathering point of the community is liturgical, and until you allow those people to preside at the liturgical functions, they will never completely be viewed as the pastors or the spiritual leaders of the communities.

In many ways people still view the priest as pastor, and they view me as the administrator. In some ways they would view me as the leader of the parish, the overseer, but it's a little different than the spiritual leader. To truly allow people like myself to be pastor, you'd have to allow them to be ordained and to preside in some fashion.

It is no wonder that some of the strain for a married leader is related to his role in the liturgy of the Mass, in particular the role of preacher. Although it was not uncommon practice for the priest and pastor to rotate, so that each man preached every other weekend, the tension was evident in those parishes where the married man's preaching opportunities were minimal or nonexistent. A visiting priest mentioned the issue of the priest's liturgical role, an important agenda item for his local priest personnel board:

One of the biggest issues that we are working on is that whole question of what is their [the married leaders] role liturgically. I think that touches lots of different issues about priesthood, canonical issues, theological, sacramental issues, that are very sacred and very dear to my heart, and my life.

The understanding between this priest and his parish leader was that whenever the priest was celebrating Mass, he would deliver the homily. The only occasions when the married leader preached to his congregation was on Friday mornings when the priest was absent and he conducted a word and communion service outside the Mass. Parishioners stated that their married pastor had a real gift for preaching, but only a handful of them could attend the Friday liturgy because it was a workday.

A parishioner later described to me how this same priest worked with the married leader during the funeral services for her grandmother. She said that the priest presided at the funeral Mass and delivered the sermon, but the lay leader presided at the wake and led the prayer service for his deceased parishioner.

When I attended the Sunday Masses in this parish I watched the pastoral administrator, dressed in suit and tie, introduce the newcomers, then lead the congregation in singing the hymns while playing his guitar. In fact the Mass began with the sound of the parish leader's voice as he greeted the parishioners in front of the altar, and his voice was the last they heard, when he made the final announcements about parish activities. Throughout the Mass he was seated in the sanctuary next to the priest, and both chairs were placed on the same level. Inclusive language was stressed throughout this service, and to this end, the prayers, readings, and hymns were modified. For instance, in the readings for that day the word "ancestors" was substituted for "fathers," and "one" was substituted for "man."

A slightly different configuration occurred at a large parish where three Masses were celebrated each weekend. At all three Masses I observed the married lay leader, dressed in an alb, processing together with the priest into the body of the church. He sat right next to the priest during the ceremony, but at all three Masses, when it was time for the sermon, it was the layman who preached, not the priest. The church was overflowing with parishioners at the Sunday Masses, the singing was lively, and there was a high level of involvement on the part of the parishioners. At one of the Masses, there was a special area in the front of the church where some of the pews were reserved for parishioners who were hearing impaired, and two different women took turns signing for them all during the ceremony.

When the married leader is a deacon, however, the boundaries between the liturgical roles of priest and parish leader during Mass are more blurred. In this situation a Catholic visitor from a parish where there are no deacons could mistake this ceremony for a concelebrated Mass with two priests presiding. I witnessed such a Mass one Sunday in a parish where the deacon assisting the priest wore his alb and stole as he processed to the altar walking side by side with the priest. At the beginning of the Mass it was the deacon who greeted the people, announced the names of parishioners with birthdays that week, and they stood while the congregation applauded. He also introduced visitors who stood for another applause. During the Mass the deacon recited the prayers designated for deacons, read the Gospel, preached, helped the priest distribute communion, and made final announcements at the end of Mass. There is no doubt that the priest played the leading role on that occasion, but the deacon, who played a supporting role, had a strong liturgical presence throughout the ceremony.

A priest located in a Native American village described how he tended to "give more than what the rubrics allow" to the deacon during the Mass:

> I allow the deacon to do everything from the introduction to the opening prayer. And then usually I would expect the deacon to read the Gospel in their language. I try to let the deacon have as much involvement in the memorial acclamation, the Lord's Prayer, the sign of peace, the Lamb of God prayer, and the dismissal…all done in [their native language].

Lay parish leaders were more restricted than deacons with regard to liturgical roles. One of them explained that he performed some sacristan duties like preparing the altar, lighting the candles, and reading the epistle, but he never preached on Sundays. On occasion, however, the priest would invite him to preach during a weekday Mass. Also, when the layman brought up the idea of their sitting side by side in the sanctuary during Mass, the priest agreed to do so. He told me during our interview that he would not have initiated the practice himself because, in his view, it had to come from the parish leader.

In another parish the lay leader sat in the second row of the church with his wife and son during the Sunday Mass. He came up to receive the gifts at the offertory procession, helped to distribute communion, and made some announcements at the end of the liturgy, but that was the extent of his participation on the altar during Mass. Likewise, another lay leader sat in the sanctuary only on those occasions when he was the preacher; otherwise he sat in a pew with his family. But he said he made it his practice to greet the parishioners in the back of the church before and after Mass, "so that I am visible to people that way."

On the other hand, there was one small parish I visited where the priest read the Gospel on Sunday, but then moved out of the pulpit so that the lay leader could take his place and deliver the sermon. The parish leader held the attention of his parishioners throughout his sermon because he applied the gospel reading to the everyday lives of his people. Later, when it was time for the kiss of peace, the priest and parish leader both walked up and down the aisles, and called each parishioner by name as they shook hands and said, "May the peace of Christ be with you."

It should not be surprising to discover that on occasion there is a difference of opinion about liturgical roles, especially with regard to preaching. A lay leader described how he and the sacramental minister resolved a stressful situation regarding the role of preacher at a first holy communion Mass. The priest suggested that it would be appropriate for the parish leader to preach on this occasion. However, the parish leader, who was trained in liturgy, countered with a proposal that the woman who prepared the children for first communion should be the preacher. In fact, he confessed that he had already asked her to preach on that occasion. When the priest questioned this action, the parish leader quoted from the general instructions from the Roman Missal and the directory for Eucharist for children:

> It says that it's okay to do this. "Anyone may address the children." So I showed it to him. He still wasn't happy with it. And we haven't done it since. But she preached that day.

Their solution is an example of a parish leader who was initiating a degree of stress into his relationship with the priest because he was, in effect "pushing the margins" of his role in the parish.

Another married leader, trained as a missionary, spoke about the importance of preaching a vision:

> I am like another parishioner, sitting on the side. I do not have any visible leadership role within the Eucharist itself, and especially in the giving of the homily. You can't communicate your own vision, and this is what a leader has to be. Here we are with this sense of the vision of outreach, of community involvement, of ecumenism. And the fifteen to twenty minutes that you could get in preaching a message on that to try to get people open to that is not there, because we have a priest preaching about football and his parents.

He also reflected on other aspects of the priest's sermons:

> If you've got a dour face and you get up there and you complain about all these people who aren't here today, that doesn't help. Being able to smile and welcome people and being upbeat and caring and that kind of thing is also a part of leadership.

An incident occurred during my visit to a parish that illustrates the consequences of uncharted territory. This took place in a parish situated in a remote area of the country where the only weekly Mass occurs on Wednesday evenings, and on Sunday there is a word and communion service with the married leader as presider. On the weekend when I was visiting this parish, a real estate agent phoned the married leader and said that he had a priest in his office from out-of-state who was interested in buying some land in the area, because he wanted to retire there eventually. The priest then took the phone, told the parish leader that he was happy to discover that there was a Catholic community in that vicinity, and offered to say Mass on Sunday. The offer was accepted, with the understanding that the parish leader would be the one to give the sermon.

On Sunday the parish leader introduced the vacationing priest, and then made some announcements before the Mass started. During the liturgy he also read the Gospel and then, as planned, proceeded to preach. He had the full attention of the congregation throughout his sermon because he linked it to the gospel reading and gave illustrations from the everyday lives of his parishioners. He shared his insights with his congregation in a straightforward and loving manner. After he finished and sat down, there was a moment of silence before the priest abruptly stood up said, "Well, now, I realize that he has given a sermon, but I'd like to talk about prayer." He then proceeded to preach about the "four Rs" of prayer and told a story that had little relationship to his theme. Later during Mass, when the congregation held hands while praying the Our Father, the priest made no attempt to join hands with the parishioners. The priest's actions and demeanor exemplifies the "uncharted waters" of liturgical roles.

By contrast, I heard a very different view about this evolving role from a priest who reported that the lay pastoral administrator and he performed all of the baptisms and funerals together, and shared the prayers at the anointing of the sick. The priest then made this affirming statement: "We work as a team whenever we can. After all, he is the pastoral director." I observed their division of roles at a Sunday Mass where the married leader, wearing an alb, processed in from the back of the church with the priest. Because he was to give the sermon at all three Masses, he sat next to the priest on the altar, but preaching was his only formal role in the liturgy. He delivered the sermon in a lively manner, and it was well received by the congregation. After Mass was over, he greeted many of the parishioners outside the church, calling many of them by name.

Given the extensive traveling involved for many of these priests, it was not uncommon for the married leader to preach at baptisms, weddings, and funerals, and to be the presider at wakes and graveside ceremonies in these parishes. In cases where there were few Catholics in the family, they preferred not to have a Mass, so the priest was not obliged to officiate.

Invisibility of Lay Parish Leaders

Another aspect of ritual leadership is the question of clothing, and in particular the option of wearing an alb on the altar. On one Sunday when I attended three Masses in one of these parishes, I noticed that the lay leader wore a suit and tie in the sanctuary. Even at the third Mass, where he delivered the sermon, he did not wear an alb. He told me later that he intends to stay with that strategy as much as he can. In fact, he said that for a long time he did not even own an alb, until he decided to buy one when he was invited to participate in an interdenominational liturgy. He explained that they wanted to have the ministers and priests together, and everyone else on the altar would be wearing liturgical vestments, so he broke down and bought the alb.

A priest described a harmonious relationship with his married leader:

> I would say he does a good job, and part of that is that there are rather clear-cut delineations of whose task it is. He does things that are actually not priestly, and yet are time consuming. He doesn't interfere with the sacerdotal rubrics; he's not trying to change the Mass. He does the hard work of trying to raise money, trying to refurbish the church.

An assisting priest in another parish complained about the invisibility of the married leader during the Mass. This was in a large parish where there was one Mass on Saturday evening, three on Sunday, and three or four priests took turns covering the four Masses each weekend. One of the priests, referring to the pastoral administrator, said,

> Well, it's just that he never said anything and all of a sudden he started not showing up at all of them [the Masses]. And I go out there, and I do all four Masses, and he's the head of the parish. Why isn't he out there in front?

When I observed and participated during the Saturday evening Mass at the parish mentioned above, I noticed that the married leader's participation was, indeed, peripheral. He processed in as one of the two altar servers, but other parishioners made the announcements. Very few of the two hundred people present at that liturgy joined in the singing. Some parishioners took an active part by taking up the collection, making announcements, and helping to distribute the hosts, but there was not a strong experience of community spirit during that Mass.

Similarly another parish leader was almost invisible during Mass. He was not there to greet people as they arrived at the church, and though he went up to light the candles on the altar, he did not sit in the sanctuary during Mass. I was also puzzled by the fact that he made none of the announcements before or after Mass, contrary to what I had witnessed in almost every other parish. It was only toward the end of my visit that I learned he had dyslexia.

By contrast, there were parishes where the assisting priest and parish leader operated as a team for liturgical services. One lay leader explained how he and the priest performed baptisms and funerals together:

> We'll both have an alb on, and we've worked it out so that we each do certain parts of the baptism. I'll preach at the baptism. I'll do the introductions...the greetings, the welcomings. If it's a funeral in the church, I'll wear an alb. If it's at the funeral home or a wake service, then I don't [wear an alb]. I think, because of our relationship, that he's very comfortable with the two of us being together [in liturgical roles].

One of the assisting priests expressed his insights about the advantage of having a married person as a member of the pastoral team. He expressed his conviction that the married leader could connect better with married couples. For example, he said, "[His] reflections during his sermons bring in some of those human experiences in marriage better than I can."

Another circumstance that touches on ritual leadership occurs when the priest fails to appear for a scheduled Mass on the weekend. We turn now to look at a solution to this dilemma, commonly called "Sunday worship without a priest."

Sunday Worship without a Priest

In my earlier study I found that the unexpected absence of a priest for Sunday worship was a dilemma for the women in charge of the parishes and their parishioners. Although the official protocols for Sunday worship led by deacons and laymen were published in the 1988 Vatican *Directory for Sunday Celebrations in the Absence of a Priest*, diocesan guidelines were not available for all parishes in the United States by the fall of 1989 when I embarked on that research project. Nonetheless, on these occasions I observed that the women pastors were careful to explain to the congregation that a word and communion service was not a Mass, and invited those who wanted to leave in order to attend Mass elsewhere to do so.[1]

In 1991, however, the United States Bishops' Committee on the Liturgy published a document entitled *Gathered in Steadfast Faith: Statement on Sunday Worship in the Absence of a Priest.*[2] Consequently, when I visited twenty parishes with married male leaders in 1996–97, I found that none of them lacked guidelines for Sunday worship without a priest. Typically called a "word and communion service," this ritual consists of the following elements: introductory prayers, readings from the scriptures, a reflection on the scripture readings, and the distribution of the hosts reserved in the tabernacle that had been consecrated during a previous Mass. Hymns are usually sung throughout the service as well. The key element missing in this ritual, of course, is the Eucharist prayer.

One of the visiting priests explained,

> Most Catholics don't know the difference between the Eucharist and a communion service. In fact, when I came here, half the people were going to communion services, because even when the priest is there, they [the priests] go up and get old hosts out of the

tabernacle, and give them communion from some other service.

Well, the doctrine from Vatican II says you should use the hosts of the celebration. The Eucharist is an action. We focus so much on the magic moment, and the changing of the bread and wine. Most Catholics really don't know that [at this moment] the people are offering themselves as bread and wine, and they're being transformed. And that we're receiving back what we ourselves offer.

One of the assisting priests helping out in a remote parish described the word and communion service that occurred quite often on Sundays: "We don't have fresh bread, we've got stale bread." On the other hand, he also stressed the importance of that Sunday gathering as a way to celebrate the outreach efforts in the life of the community. He added, "But I think their stale bread is adequately satisfying because it's an integral part of their life. [In that service], "The leader can lead them into ministry, and bring the ministry back."

One scenario was worked out by the priest and parish leader at the very beginning of their relationship in the parish. The married leader explained,

Father…and I got together as pastoral leaders and decided that if you cannot get another priest to come and fill in, we would have a Sunday liturgy of the word with communion. We would let people know the week before if that was possible, through the bulletin, and Father would announce at the Sunday liturgy that the following weekend, I would be presiding at Sunday Liturgy of the Word with communion, which would take the place of their Sunday worship services. I led two of those. I used the first minute or two after the opening song to tell the people, "I am not a priest. My role is pastoral administrator. I'm appointed by the bishop to do things like this, and this service will take care of your Sunday worship experience." I tried to make it a teachable moment for the people, saying, "This is not the way we want things, but it's the way we need to gather as people to celebrate God's love for us."

Although the priest was typically scheduled for the Sunday Mass, sometimes he failed to inform the parish that he was unavailable. A married leader of an African American parish described his experience:

> I can remember one occasion when that happened. [The assisting priest] was out of town and had scheduled a priest in his place. For whatever reason, the priest didn't show up and so I said to the congregation, "There's no priest to celebrate Mass. For whatever reason, this person hasn't arrived. We're going to go ahead and have church." And we did, and so we had procession, we had opening songs, we had scripture reading, and we had communion. And so, you know, we had church.

It was more typical for parishioners to have a communion service on weekdays in these parishes, because the priest usually came only on Sundays to celebrate Mass for them. I learned how important these gatherings were for the solidarity of the parish. As a longtime member of a poor barrio parish explained,

> We have been attending a communion service on Wednesdays, on a weekly basis, because we do not have a priest. But that has been going on for as long as we haven't had a priest. And myself and my husband, we

have always participated in the Wednesday service. To us, it's just as important as going to Mass.

Although participation in a community liturgical service was important to this parishioner, she was well aware that it was not a celebration of the Mass.

Priest Burnout: An Inside View

All of the priests in this study were driving round-trip every weekend to celebrate Mass and administer other sacraments at these parishes, and each of them had at least one full-time assignment in another location, with the exception of one elderly priest who was chronically ill. My research focuses on an inside view of what goes on inside some of these parishes. It is important to note that the total number of parishes throughout the United States without resident pastors has continued to grow, from 236 in 1990 to 782 by 2000.[3] Given the time constraints on these priests, it is inevitable that conflict and strains would arise when a person works well over forty hours per week.

A case of burnout that stands out in my mind is a tall, strong-looking, middle-aged priest, who had three years of service as a marine, two of them in Vietnam, before he went into the seminary. At the time of our interview he had been a priest for eighteen years. On Sundays he would say Mass at his own parish, and then drive forty miles over country roads to say Mass and hear confessions at a parish entrusted to a married layman. Although he did not use the term "burnout," he described his over two-hour round-trip trek each Sunday as hard and exhausting:

Sunday afternoons I just go back to the house and collapse. People sometimes will ask you to go out to eat or something like that. Very often right after Mass on

Sunday, I don't want to go anywhere. I want to crawl up and sleep somewhere. It's not that I'm unhappy. I'm just exhausted. It drains you.

He said that some of the parishioners had expressed a desire to have Mass during the week, but he said, "We haven't done that yet. Forty miles is a long way. It's kind of a hard trip to make."

This same priest also described some of the ways that he avoided burnout. When the parish initiated a building program, he came to a couple of the planning meetings, and participated in the discussion, but he questioned how involved he should be in this process. For two reasons he backed off and stopped driving in for the meetings:

One was that it was necessary for him, as leader of the community to pull this off and do this with the people. And secondly, was the idea of my area of responsibility, where my boundaries are. I'm a big one on boundaries to a certain extent. In the Marines we always had what you'd call a TAOR. That's for Topographical Area Of Responsibility, and that's what you took care of. And I kind of function that way. I'm a parish priest, I do my thing here. I know a lot of priests who run all over the diocese doing all kinds of things, involved in every kind of committee you can think of, and they love it. Not me. That's where burnout comes from. You've got to cut that off and say "This is what I am. I'm not this." You've got to identify it real quick.

Some older priests volunteered to help out as sacramental ministers in these parishes, but physical and emotional exhaustion and other health problems limited their activity. A case in point was that of a retired priest who drove fifteen miles each way to help out in a rural parish. It was his practice to say the evening Mass on

Saturday, and then make the trip back to his home. On Sunday morning he would drive back to the parish, celebrate Mass and hear confessions before returning home. His labored breathing was evident throughout the Mass that I attended. During our interview, I asked him why he didn't stay overnight at the rectory on Saturday evenings so that he could cut down on his driving time. He explained that he was suffering from emphysema, and he made the trip back on Saturday because he needed to be hooked up to his respirator at home each evening. He continued,

> I have scar tissue building up on my lungs, and I really don't have any air sacs. They're collapsing, too. My father bent over to turn off the TV and dropped dead. And my sister went to bed, pulled up her covers, folded her hands, and she died.
>
> He smiled as he concluded, "So I'm always very careful not to fold my hands!"

Another priest, who had been ordained for fourteen years at the time of our interview, said that he made the forty-mile trip from his own parish to the parish headed by a married deacon about four or five times a week. He said Mass four times a week at both churches and attended meetings of the parish council and the finance council in each parish as well. He expressed his concern about some priests in his diocese who were burning out because they helped out at two or three other parishes. He was especially worried about some of the younger priests, ordained for less than five years, who were quitting or going on sabbaticals because, in his words, "They were over used."

An elderly priest who was retired, but helped out as a sacramental minister, reported that on Sunday mornings he would leave at 7:30, and return home after all the Masses were said at about 1:30, unless there were other commitments. For example, on the previous Sunday, he could not leave immediately after the last Mass, because a couple approached him and asked him to bless their marriage on the occasion of their anniversary. It was the married leader of that growing parish who summed it up by saying, "We're going to kill the priests that we do have because we're going to need more and more Masses and they're getting older and older."

One of the pastoral administrators reiterated the rationale that was conveyed to the parishioners regarding his appointment as parish leader:

> It was presented as, "The priests are getting worn out, and one of the reasons they're worn out is because they have to do the business things: the school board, the pastoral council. They've got to go to all these meetings and we want to let them just concentrate on the sacramental [aspects]. So if we have [a pastoral administrator], the priests are actually going to be more free to see you when you're in the hospital, to do sacramental things." So a lot of people said, "Oh, that's better because father's more available when I need him." They don't care if father skips all those meetings.

The wife of a parish leader talked about her husband's frustration in his search for a sacramental minister to help out in a remote rural area:

He had a priest from [another town] that seemed like a possible candidate, who understood the mission, understood that we weren't asking him to be pastor, and that sort of thing. And he ended up going into alcohol treatment a few weeks before getting started with helping us.

A priest who had served as pastor of two parishes for a time before a pastoral administrator was put in charge of one of them, described his former situation:

My original Sunday schedule was 8:30 Mass at [Church A], 9:30 Mass at [Church B], and 11:00 Mass at [Church A]. So I never got to stay anyplace. I was always on the run....And neither place really wanted to acknowledge that I was half-time in each one...Both parish councils demanded that I spend three days a week in one, four days a week in another.

When I asked him if they demanded that he stay overnight at both places, he laughed and replied,

Yeah, and like a fool, I did it....had stuff in both places. You know, wherever I had Mass, the night before, I'd be there. If I did it again, I wouldn't have a residence in either place. The danger is though, when you don't live in a place, that you don't bond with the people.

Eight of the priests in my study lived alone. Another was living in his mother's home, and was her sole caregiver. Only eleven of them could be described as "living in community with his brother priests." The "living alone" phenomenon, a great concern of the bishops I interviewed, is discussed in the following chapter.

One of the parishioners in this same parish said that the assisting priest was "very big into the counseling and guidance part of his profession." And she speculated that these extra hours extended his workday to "sometimes eighteen or nineteen hours."

In one parish a retired priest was appointed as the sacramental minister. The parish leader explained,

He stayed on for a while, but he was honest about not having the energy, and would feel guilty about not being there, but this was our reality. So early on we started doing things together. And he was empowering

in the sense of [telling me to] "Do the Good Friday
service."

On that occasion the parish leader, left to his own devices,
consulted the Sacramentary to see what he could and couldn't do
in such a service, and then contacted the priest, who assured him
that he had it right. And, as the young man remarked, "That was
his in-service training."

Another problem voiced by many of the married leaders was
the difficulty of finding a substitute when they wanted to go on
vacation. In one of the parishes a former priest volunteered to
help out by leading a word and communion service.

One assisting priest talked about the opposite side of the
coin: the problem of burnout for the married leader:

> My greatest concern for him is burnout. I think he
> could go on for quite a while...for the sake of continu-
> ity. That's why the work has to be divided because I
> know how people burn out...and I've seen how it hap-
> pens with priests. The whole structure has got to be
> rearranged.

One of the conditions under which priests experience
burnout could be labeled role overload. An example of this comes
from a priest who was the pastor of two parishes, a spiritual director for priests, a preacher for parish missions throughout the diocese, and a member of two diocesan committees:

> A typical week is all the liturgical stuff...Masses on
> weekends in both places and Mass every day of the
> week except for my day off. And then I carry a large
> counseling load. Ninety percent of that is parishioners.
> I visit the school and make hospital visitations.

Another visiting priest spoke about the situation of a priest friend of his who was the pastor of two parishes:

> Both of us have said, "This is a short-term solution that's going to kill us. And then they're going to have to face the issue. Because it's ridiculous. Because you really can't be bonded to communities. It's not possible. When you're doing that, you're exhausted. You really can't minister.

Another example of role overload was an assisting priest whose full-time job was in the chancery office where he served on three diocesan committees, and all of these roles required a lot of traveling. He added, "I'm also the head of the sexual misconduct team, which is the hardest part of my job."

Only one of the visiting priests in my study had a school in his own parish, a situation that was a double burden for him. He was very involved in his parish grammar school, and said that he felt disconnected with the other parish community, where he was the sacramental minister. He admitted that he didn't feel good about the disconnection, but could not do more in that parish. Consequently, he realizes that he's not as much support for the pastoral administrator as he'd like to be, but in his view he really cannot do more than he is already doing. He explained,

> I'm more disconnected. When I go over there, I sort of pop in and do what I'm supposed to do, and then leave. I always have many other things on my mind. In a sense I'm beginning to feel that I want to get this over with.

The married leader in this same parish indicated that he had picked up on the priest's nonverbal expressions regarding his role in the parish. He said that when the priest arrives at the parish for

Mass, he nods and smiles, but he doesn't really connect with the parishioners. And, he added, "Sometimes he doesn't even smile."

Parishioners like the following expressed their concern about the role overload of priests in their diocese:

> They're too overworked. They cannot be all things to all people. And if there were more pastoral life direc-tors, to allow the priests to do the sacramental ministry, I think they'd welcome it. But the bishop is a little scared, in my opinion.

A parishioner underlined the importance of her married leader's participation in the liturgy in her parish:

> I have no problem with it. I think, "Thank God we've got him." Because it does help the priests. And I've seen priests burned out, more than once. So I thank God for [him].

The issue of isolation was also introduced by some of my interviewees. A married leader voiced his concerns about the iso-lation of priests, in particular, those who were living alone in a rectory:

> You don't get away from work. I talked to a number of priests, and I do know a number who are living "off campus" if they want. But that solves one part. I think the other problem would still be isolation. And I think that needs to be addressed. Somebody in the diocese needs to be responsible for these guys…Whether it's going out for lunch or supper. But somebody's got to really make a conscious effort to meet them on their turf and see how they're doing. It's easy to get caught up with what you're doing and just stop going to meetings.

And once you do that, then it's hard to get going again, in terms of interaction.

There are some signs that diocesan offices are waking up to the challenge. An article published in 1996 contained these recommendations:

The gifts, limits, needs and morale of priests need more attention, even though pastors will be in much shorter supply. New formulas and standards for maintaining smaller parishes must be found, lest the shortage of priests force parishes to close prematurely. At the same time, priests cannot become circuit riders for impersonal celebrations of the Eucharist.[4]

As we will see in the next chapter, several of the bishops were not only aware of the growing isolation of priests, but they also counseled their priests about creating communal living arrangements.

Stressful Relationships

Cultural differences between priests and married leaders were also sources of strain in some of the parishes I visited. A Hispanic deacon said,

In looking at a priest, you give him a measure of respect for who he is and what he's capable of doing. And when these priests look at me as a deacon, and as a Hispanic deacon, I guess they sense somebody's who's ignorant, uneducated, incapable of anything. I've had Anglo priests come and say, "I did not know you could give a homily like that." They can't see a Hispanic as a professional, as a public speaker, as a professional, as an administrator. That's a threat.

He also said that he had talked to Hispanic priests who "recognize and feel the separateness that exists, even in the brotherhood of priests, between the Anglo priests and the Hispanic priests."

An assisting priest in a Native American village who saw himself as a visitor within a different culture said,

> It's a real struggle, because I'm just two years ordained. I'm a white visitor, even though I have a privileged position within the village. I'm still a visitor within this culture. And I'm looking back and seeing how we've hurt the native cultures. We've made some of the apologies…like the drum dancing got pushed underground or into silence for so many years until a few brave people, Jesuits and others, said there was nothing wrong with this. And the drumming and the dancing came back. And so it's a real struggle for me.
>
> How does the message of Christ in its richness transfer to a community that's so rich in many ways, and yet still needs to hear about healing and compassion and forgiveness? I guess forgiveness is something I talk about a lot.

He concluded,

> I love being out there, but I hate the travel. You get pulled in so many ways. The idea is you're a sacramental minister, you're not the pastor. You're letting the native person who's doing it make the mistakes, and make the right choices. So you can't stick around a lot. You have to get out, and go to the next village.

Given the fact that the assisting priest is typically overextended and has little time to iron out differences that arise between him and the married leader, I was not surprised to hear about instances of tension in this relationship. The friction between a married deacon and his assisting priest was personified when I watched the priest's reactions to the latter's sermon one Sunday. The priest, who was sitting in front of the altar facing the people, sent out some nonverbal signs that he was not engaged in the sermon. Though he seemed to be listening intently at the beginning, he soon began to look down at the floor, to put his hand to his mouth in order to muffle a yawn now and then, and even looked like he was sleeping at one point. Like many sermons, it could have been shortened, but the priest's demeanor, visibly showing his lack of enthusiasm for the message, did not signal an endorsement of the speaker's authority.

Another priest described a difficult relationship with his parish leader, who was totally dedicated to his parishioners, but ambivalent about his position in the parish:

> I'm so frustrated. He's quitting one day. He's not quitting [another day]. At a team meeting I said [to him], "You have to get off the pot. You have to decide. Either resign or don't resign because we can't take this constant ambivalence." And the ambivalence is in his own heart.

Because the sacramental minister's role is an evolving one, and the parishioners were accustomed to having their own resident pastor, it was essential that the boundaries and expectations be clearly spelled out for both parties. Some of the dioceses had prepared the parishes by sending the bishop or his representative to make a formal presentation to the parishioners in order to explain the rationale for this change in leadership before it took place. Other dioceses had also prepared guidelines that were distributed to the parishioners prior to the time that their new leader arrived. It was in those places where little preparation was made beforehand that more stressful relationships emerged in the parish community. One of the parish leaders explained,

> Father...didn't have a job description until he had been doing it for six months. Then he called up and said, "I have to start coming to the spiritual life and worship committee meetings, because I'm supposed to be giving input on liturgical stuff." So, there's sort of a confusion there.

By contrast, a visiting priest showed me his letter from his bishop, which stated:

> As you are aware, Deacon...is pastoral administrator in...and Deacon...administrates this parish on a day-to-day basis. You are appointed to the position of canonical pastor. It is your responsibility to provide general supervision and especially sacramental services.

This bishop also gave clear evidence of his support for the deacon by sending a representative from the chancery office to his parish to make a formal announcement to the parishioners. The deacon described the occasion:

> He came down and made the announcement the week before I was actually going to take over. He read a letter from the bishop, and then he spoke briefly about what my responsibilities were going to be. He did explain that this was an appointment by the bishop. It wasn't something that I had elected to do, but that I had been asked by the bishop, and I had accepted.

An assisting priest in a Native American village described how he was "stared down by the elders" at a parish council meeting when the issue of a change in the scheduled time for the Sunday Mass was discussed. The elders won out because, as the priest described it,

> Well, when I have five of the respected elders staring at me, I have to do this. [The Native American pastoral administrator who is also the tribal leader] is just sitting there, and won't say anything, except being translator for me. Well, it's more than being caught between a rock and a hard spot.

One of the married leaders described his assisting priest as "ecumenically insensitive." He explained,

> We will sometimes have several guests in the church on Sunday who are Baptists. And he gets up there and gets big into Mary or something that is really off the wall as far as the Baptists are concerned....There are times when I wish that he would take more time to explain, instead of just jumping into it. I know that they [the Baptists] must be thinking, "Gee, these people are worshiping Mary." Which is what they accuse us of, and it would help if he would at least explain. I've talked to him about this, and he feels like I'm caving in. I don't see myself as caving in so much as reaching out. But I see him as more of a triumphalist.

One of the deacons described a meeting of priests, deacons, and laity who were parish leaders. He compared two types of mindsets of the priests regarding married parish leaders that he perceived at that meeting:

> I know there's a lot of priests that are threatened. They feel like, "Who do you think you are? We went through

all these classes and sacrifices and suffering and all this to make it where we are, and you didn't have to go through any of that. So why should you have any of the rewards that are really meant for us?" It's like last Sunday's Gospel. "Why should this guy that came in at the end of the day get as much pay as the rest of us, who have been working since the beginning?" But I see in that room there are so many [priest] pastors that are ready to take me in. They're ready to help in whatever situation I need.

The deacon's words, "They're ready to help," indicates another type of priests' strategies that were sustaining and encouraging for these married leaders, in contrast to the aforementioned inhibiting factors. We turn now to a discussion of types of support: "troubleshooting," mentoring, and inculcating positive attitudes in those who collaborated with these married leaders.

Priests' Support for Married Leaders

Because of their close working relationships with the parish leaders, the assisting priests were in a unique position to spot problem areas, and to aid in solving them. In one of the two parishes in my study where the married man was not a collaborative leader, it was the sacramental minister who was able to analyze the situation and work toward a resolution of the problem. He said he was aware that people were beginning to leave the parish after the new leader's appointment, and some were going to other parishes for religion classes because "they didn't like the program at their own parish." He voiced his concern that this particular parish leader was not a strong representative of the parish:

I would say that he could go to more deanery meetings than he goes to. And I would criticize him for that. I think it's important that he goes to deanery meetings, and he misses quite a few of them.

At the conclusion of this interview, the priest said he expected that the parish administrator would move before his term was up, and possibly by the following summer, because "There's something wrong. I don't know what it is. I haven't put my finger on it....He just doesn't fit." In fact this priest analyzed the situation correctly. Less than a year after he uttered these words, the pastoral administrator resigned.

Another example of troubleshooting comes from a priest who voiced his concerns about the psychological health of the parish leader in a remote rural area, and described his mediating role:

He suffers from depression at times. And it's exacerbated when he doesn't take care of himself. And in one of those episodes last summer, we got real frank here on the couch about, "Is it time for you to move to another place?" And he was, at that point, ready.

A former priest pastor was singled out as an advocate by a married leader:

I think the previous pastor set some real good groundwork for my arrival. Not just think, I know he did. He was very, very supportive. He paved the way for my coming. This parish was used to lay preaching and lay leadership. Our music director is a Lutheran minister. Married, has a family. He's been visible in terms of preaching, like on ecumenical Sunday. They're used to married people in some kind of leadership.

Another example occurred during the screening process for applicants applying for the job of pastoral administrator. An older and conservative priest who was about to retire asked the candidate, "What do you intend to do to correct the mistakes of Vatican II?" The question stunned the other priests and lay members of the interviewing team, but the candidate handled the question so well that the priests and laity on the team agreed that he should be hired for the job.

Some parishioners in my study of women parish leaders used the strategy of attempting to make an end run around the lay pastor by treating the assisting priest as the one in charge of the parish. In contrast to the women, these male parish leaders looked and sounded like priests. Interestingly enough, I found that the end run strategies also occurred in some of these parishes headed by men.

In both situations it was extremely important that the priest tackle the problem on the spot by reminding the parishioner that he was not the one in charge of the parish, and would therefore refuse to participate in an attempt to undermine the authority of the parish leader. As the assisting priest in a parish entrusted to a married layman said, "They'll ask for me and I refer them to him, because I don't want to take over the parish. That's his job."

Another assisting priest said,

> I do my very best to be around after Mass and to greet people, so they can feel that there is a priest connected to the parish. But they've learned very quickly and very well that they don't come to me. They go to [the married leader].

It was important that the priest support the authority of the married man in charge of the parish; otherwise a parishioner could successfully maneuver an end run strategy and jeopardize parish harmony. One of the priests explained the difference between the mindsets of priests who were pastors and in charge of their parishes and priests who were assisting priests (called pastoral life directors in his diocese): "When a diocesan priest becomes a pastoral life director, the buck stops with the lay pastoral coordinator, not with the priest." The married leaders cited several incidents of this strategy. One of them summed it up this way: "When people come to him with a problem that really belongs to me, he said, 'You need to talk to [the parish leader] about that.'"

Another lay leader explained that the parishioners had, in the past, gone to the sacramental minister if they had a problem. But their new visiting priest's response is, "Well, I'm sorry. Talk to [the married leader]. I'm not in charge of this parish."

The wife of a deacon told me that her husband's assisting priest was one who "knew his place," and was very supportive. She described an occasion when a parishioner introduced the priest as the pastor. The priest immediately said, "Oh, no! [Deacon...] is the pastor. I'm not the pastor."

As I mentioned earlier, there was one parish where a former pastor was in residence, but he was a semiretired priest, and was not appointed as the sacramental minister. Nonetheless, he voluntarily assisted the lay pastor by sometimes acting as a building maintenance supervisor. He said, "I call attention to things I see that need to be repaired. I take it upon myself to remind the janitor about some things." He quickly added that he always reported such interactions with the janitor to the parish leader.

One of the married leaders spoke about the mentoring role of his sacramental minister:

> My assisting priest and I work very well together. I think it's a good fit. I can certainly consult him. I rely on his wisdom. He's been a pastor in the past, so he has some wisdom that I can draw on.

Another married leader said that he met monthly with the priest who was assigned to be his immediate supervisor. He described these meetings as informal and helpful, and explained, "We have good rapport, and it's more like just bouncing issues back and forth."

A parishioner in another parish said,

> I think he and Father…, they complement each other perfectly. They're side by side. It's not one's up here and one's down there. They're very equal, and they're very equal to all of the parishioners.

A priest who was new to the role of assisting priest said,

> It's a general rule that I tend to follow, that the first year you don't change anything. And in this case I might not change anything the second or third time. [laughs] I mean that's a part of the whole new arrangement, too. I just say [to the married leader], "What do you want?"

An example of on-the-job mentoring came from a married leader:

> He [the priest] came over to the church and walked through things with me and said, "Do this. Try this. Use incense in this way." All those real hands on, practical things, that nobody else had done.

One of the assisting priests described how he and the parish leader coordinated their visits to the sick and homebound parishioners. The priest began by taking him along to visit each one of the parishioners on his route. There, as the married man described it, "The first thing he does, whenever he sees somebody, he grabs me and says, 'I want you to meet our parish director.' He's very, very supportive." After the initial visits, they divided the calls into two geographical sectors, and took turns making home calls in each sector, so that all of the homebound were visited once per month.

Another parish leader who chaired the parish council meetings explained that if his assisting priest had something he wanted to bring up to the parish council, he would bring it to the parish leader, who would then bring it up at the next council meeting. But when the priest came to the meetings, he made it clear by his words and actions that it was not he, but the parish leader, who was the one in charge.

The wife of a parish leader spoke of the support shown to her husband by the former assisting priest.

> I thought he really gave power to [my husband]. He fully supported him, fully expected him to give half of the sermons, fully deferred to him for decisions. [My husband] made the decisions. Father would back him up. Father…was our spiritual leader and [my husband] was our pastor. It really did help [my husband], gave him so much confidence.

The designation of a parish as "without a resident priest" usually refers to a parish that is lacking a priest who lives there and serves as the pastor. One of the parishes in this study that was headed by a married man also had a retired priest in residence. The priest, mentioned earlier, was not the pastor, nor was he designated as the sacramental minister. This elderly priest had chosen to make the rectory his retirement home, because he had served as pastor there for a number of years, and was fond of the parishioners. Besides helping out with the Masses on Sunday, he regularly visited parishioners who were living in retirement homes or were hospital patients. In addition, he answered the rectory telephone in the evenings, so a more accurate description of his status would have been "semiretired." This was very helpful for the married leader, whose home was located outside the parish boundaries.

The semiretired priest and the married leader had great respect for each other. The former said, "I can live with any set-up, actually, but this is good." And he added, "I personally feel that there are a lot of priests who are in good physical health who would be very smart if they would do the same type of thing." He then described another semiretired priest who helps out at a parish, but lives in a separate home in the neighborhood, and stated that he lived in a separate apartment himself for awhile, but didn't "care much about it." Why? Because, as he stated it, "I prefer being right where the action is." He also voiced his opinion of life at a rest home when he said,

> I don't want to look at four walls, and rarely go out to a parish or to visit nursing homes on Sundays. I'm part of the church this way. I know what's going on.

The married leader, who deeply appreciated the older man's wisdom, summed it up when he said, "He's been a priest for fifty-five years, so there's a lot of wealth there."

Another married leader described his assisting priest as "pretty darn pastoral" in the way he interacted with an adult parishioner who was preparing for baptism. He added,

> My suspicion is that most of the sacramental ministers do not come in as circuit riders who know nothing about the people. But they find it integral to their sacramental ministry to relate on a human level with the people with whom they celebrate the sacraments, as far as possible.

One priest described what might be termed "helpful ambivalence" regarding his relationship with the parish leader. He said that he tried to take opportunities to get together with the family.

Whenever he's invited there for dinner he goes, "because he wants to connect with them somehow." He concluded,

> I tend not to intrude into somebody else's space. And that may be for the best in this situation. I usually wait for him to ask, rather than make suggestions.

The deacon serving as the pastoral administrator in the Native American parish was also a translator for the assisting priest's homilies, because some of the elders did not speak English. Because the priest was helping out at two other missions, the deacon often presided at word and communion services in his village. I witnessed one of these services on the Sunday when I was visiting there. It was conducted entirely in their native language, the hymns were sung with great gusto, and the deacon's sermon was warmly received by the congregation. When I asked him about his role on such occasions, the deacon replied, "I feel very comfortable. I enjoy doing it."

A similar example occurred in a Mexican American parish, where the presiding priest was not fluent in Spanish. The Mexican American deacon in charge of the parish delivered a stirring homily, first in Spanish and then in English. He came down from the altar and walked up and down the aisle as he was speaking, posing questions now and then to the parishioners, and calling them each by name. For the priest, the deacon's ability to convey a message to this audience was like the role of a signer for an audience with hearing-impaired people. On that occasion I reflected on titles like parish administrator, director, or coordinator, and all seemed inadequate to describe this Mexican American leader's actual role in the parish.

In another Mexican American parish, the last priest-pastor, who had headed the parish for four years before being transferred, was instrumental in the appointment of a married deacon. He was convinced that this deacon was the natural leader of the parish, and that he would be a good pastoral administrator. So he recommended to both the bishop and the committee in charge of appointing pastors that this man should be the pastoral administrator, and the bishop and the committee accepted his recommendation.

For three of the parish leaders, their experience as seminarians facilitated their relationship with the priests of the diocese. One of them talked about the periodic meetings with twelve priests in his deanery:

> I get along well with some of them because I know them from the seminary. I know them from past experience. I mean, we have other contexts that brought us together. Those who do not know me, I haven't felt unwelcome, but I've felt some hesitation on their part. For the most part I think they are also overworked....So overall I haven't sensed any real problem.

One of the priests stressed the need for trust in joint ministry:

> When you work in a joint ministry with somebody, you've got to be able to trust and get along with that person fairly well. And to try to work hand in hand. Otherwise, you're always going to have problems.

Another assisting priest admitted that he had an ulterior motive for his positive attitude toward the married leaders in his diocese:

> There's one thing with me...Of course I've got to learn right from the beginning is, I want them to succeed. If they fold, it means...[laughs] You know who's going to have to do it!

A priest stressed the need to work as a team:

I'm here to sacramentalize for the parish. And to be a support for [the married leader]. So people know that he and I are working as a team. You can't play mom against dad here. It doesn't work. So I see myself as a sacramentalist, and that's what a lot of priests are afraid of. They don't want to turn sacramental, like you plug them in and you do it and then they leave. They don't like that. They are so afraid of becoming circuit riders. We don't want that. But I see myself as doing that in a pastoral way. That I'm here with these people.

One of the priests, a hospital chaplain, did not have a parish of his own, and he was very positive about his role as sacramental minister. He was not burnt out, nor did he resent helping out at the parish. In fact, he told me that he likes his job there, is perfectly content that he's not the pastor, and enjoys spending a lot of time at the parish. The married leader, who described himself to me as "not a people person," was not critical of the priest's presence in the parish because he valued his talents. However, the fact that the priest used the term "my beloved parish," in an article published in the parish bulletin indicates that he sees himself as the pastor of the parish, and that may be problematic for the married leader.

The Future: Visions and Strategies

Each of these priests has been working as a team with a married man and his parishioners to keep their parish communities alive and functioning. Given their unique experience, views of participants in this new church structure about the future of parish life and the means to attain that goal are instructive.

My previous study of women pastors revealed that parishioners tend to see themselves as "second-class citizens" when a nonpriest is appointed as their leader. This means that a warm welcome from the parishioners can be missing in many parishes where the priest is replaced by a married or single layperson. To alleviate this situation, one of the dioceses I visited required a year or more of internship in the parish for the men and women who were designated as potential parish leaders. During that time the future leader lived in the parish and attended all of the parish meetings with the priest until he took over the management of the parish. This practice was applauded by one of the parishioners, who said, "It was such a gradual thing that people got used to [the married leader] before he really took over." The strategy of requiring an internship period can serve as a "bridge" in the process of turning to new leaders as resources for these parishes.

In this study I discovered another form of internship that involves the expansion of the role of pastoral associate. Ordinarily the title "pastoral associate" refers to a parishioner who has the credentials to be placed in charge of a specific sector of parish life, such as youth ministry, catechetics, liturgy, or social outreach. One of the married men in my study explained how, prior to being placed in charge of the parish, he served as a pastoral associate there, and in that capacity he had been presiding at Good Friday services and burials as well as occasionally preaching at Mass. In addition it was his responsibility to enlist assisting priests to come to the parish for Mass and the other sacraments for six months of the year, because the pastor lived outside the parish in a summer vacation area where he said Masses from May until October, and during that time was not available elsewhere. In reality, then, this married man had an internship period as the parish leader for about six months per year previous to the day when the bishop appointed him as the parish leader.

A priest spoke about changes in the training of priests, and in particular a need to emphasize communication skills and grass roots experiences:

> The reality is that we end up working with pastors who are coming out of different experiences, who are not good communicators, who are not good at managerial skills....In some of the dioceses, they train them in theology for two years, then they send them out to work in a parish situation, and then they bring them back. Maybe that's a better approach.

Language was an issue in Hispanic parishes. In one diocese, located in the Southwest, the bishop said, "We're very short on Hispanic priests." He reported that there were only five or six Hispanics in their seminary, and then he laid out their two-pronged approach to alleviate this problem: Their future priests are now expected to learn Spanish in the seminary, and the diocese was working on the recruitment of religious order priests to help out in their parishes. Faced with the fact that the need for Hispanic-speaking priests greatly outweighs the supply, he concluded, "Overall, I don't know how we're going to deal with this. The Spirit's going to have to tell us what some answers are."

One of the priests voiced his concern about the future when he spoke of the proliferation of conservative seminarians in his diocese:

> One of the things that's distressing me is...among the seminarians and among the ones that seem to be going to the seminary...there's an effort to go backwards. They're much more conservative about things. You know we have some of the guys who still want to wear the cassock, which is an indicator that they still want to do everything top down. So if they're not being prepared

for mutual ministry on all levels, then I think they're in for a struggle in their future.

A sacramental minister described how his diocese was beginning to encourage their priests to articulate what they wanted to be in the future. He said they were posing questions like the following:

> "Can you have the freedom to let yourself think about whether or not you want to be a pastor?" The old model is that your affirmation comes from being named a pastor. We'd like to ask you to look at where you are going to be happiest. Are you going to be happiest with heavy administration, staff development, community development? Do you think of yourself as a teacher, preacher, as someone accompanying people on their journey?

He added that their diocese was trying to encourage seminarians to ask those questions themselves, and that it was almost like a new experience for them to think in those terms.

The restructuring process would be facilitated if the vision of this new relationship between priest and nonpriest leaders in these parishes were clarified. One of the bishops sent me a set of policy guidelines that presents a vision of teamwork between the one who "is given particular, though not in every case, exclusive responsibility within the team structure for leading the community's worship, celebrating the sacraments and fostering the spiritual growth of people" and the other who "is responsible for coordinating and administrating these and all other elements of parish life and mission." The guidelines also say that neither role "exists in isolation but in a complementary fashion. Together they represent the extension of the bishop's ministry to this portion of the local church."

One of the visiting priests presented his view of the future:

> I think lay participation is going to be always pretty
> much a factor of the church's life from now on. I think
> that's one benefit of the priest shortage. I don't see it as
> a tragedy, because I grew up in a church where the
> priests and sisters did everything....My father loved to
> do work in the church, and the priest just flat told him,
> "Look, we'll take care of that. You just get out of the
> way." See, they wouldn't let him.

A parishioner in a parish headed by a married layman said
that the majority of the parishioners in his parish realize that their
new pastor is not an interim leader. He described the "long-term
vision" for his parish: "That we will not have a resident, ordained
priest." He then added, "And if you've got a married guy with a
family, chances are he's going to be out in the community."

A priest described how he combined a "supportive" with a
"backing off" strategy in his role as sacramental minister:

> I think the relationship that [he] and I have had over the
> years has been very good. We struggle with some
> issues, some differences of opinion, but we both try to
> be sensitive to each other's needs. I hope I have been
> supportive to him. I know he's certainly been support-
> ive to me in many, many things. There are areas where
> I tend to threaten, so then I just back off. I'm not a con-
> fronter, so that's one of my weaknesses.

Another priest described his married leader as "fighting to
push the boundaries of the church out" or trying to "move things
on." He also saw this leader as one who connected better with
parishioners and who was also a bridge to other ecumenical
groups, and he confessed that those were things that he himself

didn't do very well. He said, "[The parish leader] is able to have an understanding of people's way of life a little better than some of us, meaning mainly priests. He can connect better with that than I can." For instance, he said that the parish leader's reflections during his sermons "bring in some of those human experiences in marriage better than I can." And he added, "Not only in marriage situations, but in home life in general."

The same priest stated that the priests in his diocese are positive about the married men heading parishes, but he added, "Their only negative is that they don't like to meet with non-priests when the presbyterate meets." The presbyterate, a group solely made up of priests, usually meets only once a year, and when issues about parishes are raised, the pastoral administrators are also invited to the meeting. So he sees this as a growing problem, and there is a need to take care of what he described as some "ruffled feathers," because the priests are asking, "Can't we ever meet on our own?" He concluded by suggesting that there is a need for a new vision that would provide a means for a greater sense of community among the priests of the diocese.

This priest's statement underlines the tension between the need to integrate these deacons and laymen into the pastoral life of the diocese and the need to nurture solidarity among the priests. As we will see in the next chapter, the bishops share this concern. As the number of priests living alone in their rectories continues to increase, the bishops have begun to encourage them to create community living situations for themselves. While some bishops have already begun to solve the priest shortage problem by closing parishes, others will continue their efforts to recruit and incorporate these new parish leaders into the diocesan authority structure. This means that a solution to the alleviation of the priest burnout issue should be placed on the "highest priority" list. Assigning priests to perform sacramental duties in more than two parishes, or to a second parish that requires extensive travel will, in the final analysis, only exacerbate the priest shortage.

Summary

The priests, in their role as sacramental minister, had the task of paving the way through "uncharted territories" with the parish leaders. This was especially evident in regard to such issues as preaching and ritual garments to be worn on Sundays.

After listening to the priests' experiences and their thoughts and feelings about their new role, I am most concerned about the overburdened priests who are already experiencing the burnout syndrome. The continuing decline in priestly vocations in the United States and the recent mandate regarding the dismissal of priests involved in the sexual abuse of minors will certainly exacerbate the priest shortage. This does not bode well for an alleviation of priest burnout in our country.

On the other hand, in those dioceses with longer experience and clearer guidelines regarding the roles of pastoral administrator and sacramental minister, there was less uncharted territory for both priests and pastoral administrators, and this resulted in smoother relationships between them. In particular, the parish leaders were eager to elaborate on the many instances of their priests' invaluable support as troubleshooters and mentors for them in their parishes.

Chapter 7
The Bishops:
Validation and Support

When I traveled to twenty parishes headed by women in 1989–90, I did not include interviews with the bishops who appointed these women to their new positions. This was not an oversight. At that time I deliberately avoided the bishops because I thought some might prohibit me from gathering data in their dioceses. By 1996, when I was embarking on this research effort, there were more parishes with nontraditional leadership, and my chances of scheduling interviews with bishops were greater.

In fact, the bishops were very cooperative. One of them was hesitant at first, because the new parish leader in his diocese was recently appointed. The bishop pointed out that, by the time of my proposed arrival date, he would have been on the job for only nine months. I explained that my earlier study on women parish leaders indicated how crucial that first year was for the lay leader, and equally so for the parishioners, because all of their former pastors had been priests. I stressed that we need to know more about that initial phase of the job, and the memory of this particular leader would be a lot clearer about what happened during that early stage than other parish leaders who had been heading the parish for four or five years. As soon as he heard this, the bishop graciously agreed to participate in my study.

In the end, only one bishop was not interviewed. Although he had agreed to schedule an interview with me while I was in his diocese, on my arrival I was told that the bishop had been taken to the hospital for major surgery, and shortly after my return home, I read the announcement of his death in a Catholic newspaper.

All in all, I completed nineteen interviews with bishops. Eleven bishops were interviewed about one parish I visited in their diocese, and four bishops were interviewed about two parishes. The majority of the interviews took place in the bishop's office. Other locations were a retreat house, a restaurant, and the home of the pastoral administrator. One bishop, who had agreed to an interview in his office, experienced an unexpected schedule change, and my appointment was canceled. However, he graciously consented to be interviewed by telephone after my return to Washington.

In general I would describe these interview sessions as both cordial and serious. I used my secret weapon, described earlier as "Father Joseph Fitzpatrick's rationale for research" with them at the very beginning, and once again, it proved to be an important icebreaker. In fact, as soon as I reiterated Joe's words: "To continue to unfold the mysteries of God's creation," one bishop's immediate response was, "Okay, then. So what do you want to know?"

Choosing Parishes for Alternate Leadership

Recall that canon 517.2 of church law stipulates that when there is a shortage of priests in a diocese, the bishop has the right to entrust the care of a parish to a deacon or some other person.[1] Therefore, in the first part of each interview with the bishops and the married leaders, I asked about the appointment process that was used in the recruitment of deacons and laity for this new position. Although the appointment processes were somewhat similar in the dioceses I visited, I found that there were some important differences that affected the acceptance of this married leader in his parish.

In some cases, where the parish priest became seriously ill, or was unexpectedly transferred to another parish, the appointment of the married leader was more informal and immediate.

For instance, a deacon who had been a member of the parish for a number of years, and whose appointment as a parish leader was rather sudden and informal, described it this way:

> The bishop contacted the priest who is in charge of the ordained deacons, and he's the one who actually approached me, representing the bishop, to ask if [my wife] and I would consider the appointment. He asked us about six months before the appointment. At that time, we had our house on the market and were actually thinking of moving. So it was a difficult decision. We prayed about it and talked about it and decided that we would be willing to give it a try, so that's basically how it came about.

Another bishop used the same strategy, appointing a long-time member of the parish as leader. In this case a priest pastor was moved to another parish with very little notice, and another priest was assigned to the parish, but only temporarily. A layman who had been very active in this parish described how he was appointed as the parish leader. He said that when he showed the priest around the parish the first day of his arrival, he was asked for some names of parishioners who should be considered for the position of pastoral administrator. In his words,

> I wasn't thinking of myself because I wasn't interested at the time, so I gave him some names. He asked if I was interested, and I said I was open to it. I think that's when he wrote some letters to the bishop suggesting my appointment. They called me for an interview with the bishop and the vicar general. Later on in the afternoon I got a call from the bishop or one of his assistants, asking me if I would take the job.

He then described his appointment:

I have an appointment that's a canonical appointment, and a memorandum of financial agreement between the parish and myself, signed by the bishop.

In one parish, where the priest left for another assignment, a layman who was a longtime member of the parish explained how he was appointed:

I was appointed parochial administrator pro tem for nine months. And they [diocesan officials] came down, and asked the parish to take a position like this. They [the parishioners] were a little bit scared of it and wanted a priest. So they appointed me while we had priests coming in on Sundays for about nine months. And then they appointed [Father...] as sacramental moderator, and then they officially made me parochial administrator.

Although the three parish leaders just described were appointed unexpectedly, they had been members of the parish for a number of years, and were not strangers to the parishioners. These three were among the eight parish leaders I interviewed who were members of the parish when they were appointed. The appointments were not as abrupt and informal in the other twelve parishes, because there the bishops were working with a set of guidelines adopted by the diocese before they selected the lay leaders and made the appointments.

When describing how the parishes were chosen, a bishop said,

We pick [a parish] that is open, in some way or another, to new things. I try always to tell them that we picked you because we think you're a mature enough parish to be able to be the guinea pig. That is true. We wouldn't pick a parish for a program like that if the parish was extremely difficult or impossible.

So it should be a pat on the back for them. We do that, and help them to accept it, but they're still nervous. I find they're nervous up until they get to know the new person. And then, after a couple of months, they begin to relax. And there are usually one or two key people, and if those people can be won over, then you have no problems.

Another bishop discussed the various stages of the process, and explained how the first group of parishes was assigned a parish director:

I made contact with each one of them and asked if they would be willing to be part of the experiment. Consequently I either personally or through someone else, went to the parish council with the proposal. And the parish agreed to do so.

This practice of the bishop or his representative meeting with the parish council beforehand was underlined as a "must" by another bishop, who said this:

Where there is a parish that is lifted up for having this kind of ministry, it's important for the people in authority, the bishop or his representative, to meet with the parish council. You have to meet with the parish council.

Once the parish is chosen, another way in which a bishop can be an advocate for a new leader is to prepare the parishioners for alternate leadership well before the selection process begins. As one bishop described it, this is an effort to "win over key people." He gave an example of a parish where the parish director was a laywoman, and the parishioners were not happy about it. But the chief of police, who lived in that parish, was pleased with the work she was doing. He was not only the first to accept her, but he was also the key person who subsequently convinced the parishioners to follow his lead.

The wife of a lay parish leader said, "There was a lot of education beforehand, working with the people, explaining about the transition, and so on."

A bishop in another diocese also enunciated the need for this educational process. He said,

> I am concerned that as we develop these other models and respond to real needs, that we do so in a way that respects the ecclesiology of our church. I think there needs to be a whole education process about the various roles that people will have. It can't just be announced on a Sunday morning. I think that's important; otherwise people don't understand what's happening. Humans get burnt. We need to have both sides. We need to have sensitivity and compassion.

In one of the dioceses there is a committee in charge of non-priest-headed parishes, made up of the vicar general, the vice chancellor, and a layperson. The bishop said that he consulted with his vice chancellor who chairs that committee before he chose the married man to be in charge of one of the parishes in my study. But prior to the arrival of the new parish leader, he also sent these three people down to the parish as a team. He reported, "They took a long time with the parishioners explaining the whole situation. And it turned out fine, because the people were so afraid it was going to be closed that they were willing to go along with the situation."

A married leader, who participated in some of these meetings with his bishop's team in other parishes, expressed his views in this way:

> People have to be part of the process. They have to buy into it, and they have to own it. So we asked, "Are you, as a parish, comfortable with this?"
>
> If you want it to work, and you want to make it easier for people, let them talk about it. Get all their fears out, and get the answers beforehand.

A different approach was used by another bishop who described his first meeting with parishioners of a parish that was chosen for alternative leadership:

> I met with a representative group of parishioners [parish council president, the former pastor who was leaving, a trustee, some parish council members] and I said, "We have chosen you to receive a parish director." I didn't ask for their consent, I asked for their cooperation. I explained to them why they were chosen. And they had the chance to take this information to the parish council and say, "The diocese has asked us to do this."

The following account by a parishioner is a recipe for failure:

> I don't believe that we were really told, and I think it needs to be very explicit and specific what this person's role is: What authority role did he take, what role did he have over the committees, what role did he have with respect to preaching, to the students receiving instructions during Mass. I guess we were told individually, or

within our specific groups, but I don't think there was ever a precedent set in writing that said, "This is really [his] role."

A candid bishop told of his failure to prepare the parishioners. He said,

> The unfortunate thing was that we didn't prepare the people adequately for this transition, for the fact that they were going to be without a resident priest pastor. We did not prepare them well at all. So we're trying to correct that with some new policies that will help people to understand and prepare for this eventuality.

One of the pastoral administrators described how the bishop prepared the wife and children of the married leader as parishioners-to-be in the new situation. He said that the bishop traveled to their home and talked to each of them separately. Here is his account of the questions the bishop asked his children:

> "Well, are you okay with this? Are you going to be comfortable with your dad doing this kind of stuff? What's it going to mean to you?"

The parish leader explained why these individual sessions with the members of his family were so important. Although he had been involved in committee work as a parishioner, he would soon be placed in a different position in the parish, one that had hitherto been occupied by priests. He said, "It was so new. They knew what I had been doing, but nobody was really sure what this was going to look like when they got finished."

Application, Screening, and Appointment Procedures

Once the parishes are chosen for alternative leadership, the processes of appointment to this new position and screening of candidates begins. One bishop of a large diocese who delegated an auxiliary bishop to be in charge of the parish directors, explained the process in this way:

> I set it up so there would be a committee to interview, which is in two stages. We keep a pool of names of possibilities. That's the first stage. There's a committee that does that. Then when a vacancy comes and we have decided to appoint a parish director, then another committee moves into operation, and I take whatever they surface as the best candidate.
>
> Once that occurred we had a system. We had one group called the screening committee, which has established some basic criteria, and assessed the profiles of those who applied for the position. [That committee] made recommendations as to the most promising candidates, saying, "We think for this parish this person would be the best person."

One of the lay parish leaders told me of his experience in this process:

> There was an ad in the archdiocesan newspaper, announcing that they were accepting applications for parish directors. What they were doing was creating a pool of candidates that would be available. If I wanted to get into the parish directorship at that time I needed to apply. So I went for it and sent in my papers.

In some dioceses the screening process was lengthier and more sophisticated than others. As one candidate explained,

> It was two months before I heard that they had accepted the application and that I was moving along in the interview process. A month later I met with a screening committee. There were about five or six people on that committee. It was about an hour-long interview. Questions like "Why do you want this? What qualities to you bring?"

Dioceses with a longer experience of appointing pastoral administrators tended to have more sophisticated screening processes. For instance, in one diocese, after the applications were received, the guidelines state that those considered potentially qualified are to be invited for a personal interview with a screening committee. This committee checks on areas such as personal development, values, critical thinking, communication, interaction, problem solving, global perspective, and aesthetic response.

In this diocese the qualified applicants also come together for a one-day assessment of their participation in a number of tasks. One of them is a slide selection exercise, where each participant views sixty slides of parish-related material. The task is to select out ten slides that best represent a participant's concept of parish, and to write a script to accompany the slides. Then each participant makes a presentation of their slides and script to the group. In the next exercise, the group of candidates works together to come up with one set of ten slides and draft a script to go with them. In these and other exercises during that day, collaborative and interactive skills are showcased, as well as the vision of church.

The following report is from the experience of one of the men who survived the screening:

I was notified that I was to come for a day-long screening process. And it was an intensive and interesting day. In the morning we had some group activities and some individual activities. The supervisors were watching how we work as a team, who takes the lead, those kinds of things. And we worked in two teams or as a whole team, and there were also some individual activities that we had to do.

An activity I remember was called an "in-basket activity." They had twenty-five items (letters, telephone messages, notes) in our in-basket. Supposedly we were on our first day of the job, and we had to prioritize these twenty-five items, and make a quick note as to the type of response.

The thing I remember most was that somebody interrupts you and says there's a street person at the door, and they want a handout. And the guy who interrupted me was supposed to be my secretary. And I said, "Well, go and do whatever you normally do." And the person who was role-playing as my secretary said, "Well, I don't know. I'm new here, too." So I said, "Well, call St. Vincent de Paul Society." I was really focused on wanting to get this in-basket done, because we were really under the gun in terms of the clock.

So finally the guy grabbed me by the collar and said, "No, stupid. This is a simulation! You've got to go to the door and talk to that person. You really have to do this." So he yanks me out of the chair, and we go to another room where this street person is, and I had to interact with him. And of course they watched the interaction and how you handled the situation.

He informed me that the candidates had been given prior notice about the concluding activity for the day, putting together their first word and communion prayer service that they might conduct for their new parish. They were told to "explain why and what you did in putting it together." He added, "So each of us had to get up and actually kind of do it, except we didn't go through all the prayers. We just said 'Here's the reading I would use...here's the kind of homily I might have used for that.'"

Once all of the candidates have been interviewed, the next process was the selection of candidates. An auxiliary bishop described it this way:

> Then we have what we call a selection committee, which has in mind the specific parish, and invites the candidates to sit down with the priest dean of the district and the parish consultant. This consultant is an individual diocesan person [lay man or woman] who works with the whole district....And we sit down together in order to discuss the parish, the person, and to make a determination whether we think this is really going to be a good match or not. I chair the selection committee. We have a group discussion, and then we take it to the bishop and say, "This is our recommendation."

A bishop in a diocese with a long experience in making these appointments presented his strategy regarding the range of candidates for this position:

> I wanted, from the beginning, to have as wide a spectrum as possible of parish directors. We had only four at the time. I wanted men and women, married and single, religious and lay, and an ordained deacon if possible, but I wanted the whole spectrum in order to show that this is not a gender issue, this is a competency issue. So it

started with as wide a spectrum as possible. In that first set of four people who were parish directors, we had a woman religious, we had a married woman, we had a single woman who had been a member of a religious community, and we had a married man.

One of the candidates who had gone through the selection process was called to the bishop's office, where he was offered the position of parish director, effective in one week. It was the parish where he and his wife had been active parishioners, and he accepted the position. The new parish director said that the priest who was leaving the parish contacted him and announced,

> Well, I've got everything packed. When can you come and get it? I said, "What do you mean?" And he said, "Well, July 1st you have to start signing the checks, not me." And that was my in-service to the whole thing. Two boxes. "Come and pick them up." And that's how we got started.

A bishop in another diocese described the result of his interview with a married couple applying for a parish in his diocese. He said,

> I had known them from some previous work when they were visiting the diocese. Having known them from an interview, I was quite pleased that they were applying for this position, because I felt that the two of them are deep in their faith. They love the Church, and they are trained and competent to do this kind of ministry. So I was very happy to have them.

The decreasing numbers of vocations has resulted in a smaller pool of priests available for parish work, and the shortage has also been exacerbated by a retreat from diocesan parishes by order priests. When this happened in one of the parishes included in this study, the bishop solved the problem by entrusting the parish to a diocesan priest who was the pastor in a neighboring parish. In effect, then, this priest was serving as the pastor of both parishes.

When the already overburdened priest found a deacon who was willing to help out, and informed the bishop about it, an unusual twist in the appointment process occurred. The bishop told the priest that he (the priest) could appoint the deacon as a full-time minister to take care of the daily operations of the second parish.

This deacon was the only parish leader in my study who was not appointed directly by the bishop. In this case, however, the bishop had delegated his authority to one of his diocesan priests to appoint alternative parish leadership as stipulated in church law. This occurred in a diocese where there were no written guidelines describing the duties, rights, and responsibilities regarding the role of pastoral administrator.

The bishop's decision could be interpreted as a supportive action on his part, because it showed his confidence in the priest's understanding of the sort of person needed by the parish in question. As it turned out, however, the relationship between the priest and married leader was fraught with problems from the outset because the lines of authority were unclear.

This was the first time I had heard about this type of appointment, so I asked the parish leader for a deeper explanation. He said that his diocese "does not have anything official" in making these appointments:

> This is not a canonical appointment. The only pastoral administrators in the [diocese] are those hired by the parish. To my knowledge there are no pastoral administrators named canonically by the bishop.

The visiting priest echoed the words of the married leader and elaborated:

> This is not a canonical appointment. The bishop wants us to be responsible. I talked to him about it and asked him why, because I thought this gives him no authority. The reason he doesn't want to get tied up is if somebody doesn't do a good job, he doesn't want any trouble getting rid of them. The role isn't defined yet, and I think they will define it eventually.

At the time of my visit to this parish, the married leader informed me that he had submitted his resignation, and would be leaving the parish very soon. This was not surprising, given the stressful relationship between the priest and the parish leader.

Installation Ceremonies

In my earlier study of parishes headed by women, I found that the bishop's presence on the altar during a liturgical ceremony in the parish church, where he officially installed her as the new parish leader, was a key source of validation for these women. It was also reassuring for the parishioners because his presence at the ceremony made it clear to all of the parishioners present that it was the bishop himself who had appointed this new parish leader as the head of their parish. This is the reason why I asked my interviewees about the installation ceremony.

With respect to the aforementioned parish where the priest appointed the pastoral administrator, it would have been helpful if the bishop had come to the parish and presided at a ceremony where he officially installed the married man as the parish leader, but there was no sign that this bishop intended to do so.

By contrast, the parishioners in fourteen of the twenty parishes in my study personally experienced an installation ceremony, where the bishop himself or his official representative was the presider. The ceremony usually took place during the first month after the arrival of the new leader, and the principal function of the installation is the legitimation of the new person's leadership. This is, of course, a key issue in parishes where the parishioners had never before experienced a nonpriest as parish leader.

One of the parishioners described the installation of his deacon as the head of the parish in this way:

> The bishop came and actually presented him as our pastor, which had not happened the first time we had a pastoral administrator. And he supported him in the way that he introduced him to the congregation as the pastor of the community. It was a very beautiful ceremony, and a very impressive ceremony.

The wife of a parish leader described the installation ceremony as "really nice," and testified to the bishop's strong support. She said,

> He came later that month and preached at all the Masses, to tell the people what [my husband's] role was going to be, and he said, "If I could, I would name him pastor, but canon law says I can't."

Another wife of a parish leader said that the installation ceremony was "very important." She described the ceremony, with a priest from the diocesan office who was in charge of pastoral administrators as the presider. She said,

> People needed to see someone from [the diocesan office] come. Father...came out, and Father...was also

part of it because he was being installed as the sacramental minister. We had a big pork roast afterwards for the whole parish, and the majority of the people who were at church went downstairs for it.

A deacon said that his wife and children were part of the installation, and that this ceremony showed strong support from the bishop. He added,

> Not only support, but concern. He was very open in telling the people that I had a full-time job working [outside the parish], and it was a forty-hour a week job, and they should be careful not to kill me in requiring too much of me. So he was very supportive of me, and very open in reminding them that I was now pastor for them. So he really did affirm me to the community.

A married leader who labeled his ceremony a "dual installation" said,

> I wore a white alb and was sitting next to [the priest assigned as the sacramental minister], and [the bishop's representative] at the presider's chair during the liturgy. The thing we emphasized was that it wasn't just my installation as pastoral administrator, but equally important, it was the installation of Father...as sacramental minister. So he and I both had to answer questions, like "Are you willing to serve?" And then at the reception we had a cake with both of our names...Everything was done together, which is important to me. Because people need to realize that we are going to have sacramental ministry here, but we need to work as a team.

THE BISHOPS ✦ 229

A parishioner described the participation of the members of the parish council and the use of symbols in the ceremony that took place in his parish.

> The bishop would call for the various people on the parish council. They would come up and present [the pastoral administrator] with a parish membership list, the end of the year budget balance, a copy of the parish mission statement, and other items that symbolize our parish.

When I asked a bishop in another diocese about his participation in the installation ceremony, he said,

> It's important for the administrator because it gives a sign of approval. It also allows me to say good things to them, to remind them that this is an exemplary thing, and that this is part of the wave of the future. And they should not feel in any way diminished just because they don't have a priest.

One of the six parish leaders who were not officially installed reported that diocesan officials came to his parish before he arrived. He said, "They came down here a number of times, and prepared them and talked to them about it. And then they brought me down to some meeting of the parish council."

Another "noninstalled" parish leader, who nonetheless felt that his bishop had been very supportive, explained:

> He didn't come down here with the retinue, which the installation would have involved, several people coming with him and all that kind of thing. The bishop just drove down himself. In a way, that's what it was, an installation. He just didn't say, "You're installed,"

because I'd already been here three months. But it was
the same thing.

A female parishioner in a parish where the new leader was
not installed by the bishop, said that her bishop had a "hands off"
attitude about the parish, which she respected. She explained, "I
think we're meeting some needs that aren't necessarily met at
other geographic parishes. I think the bishop stays in the background, but he lets it happen, and I think that's good."

A bishop explained his position regarding installation
ceremonies:

> I have some real mixed feelings about it. The way I see
> our ecclesiology in the church, pastoral care is first
> given to a bishop for a region, who then gives it to his
> coworkers, the priests. I would not be favorable to hav-
> ing an installation ceremony for a pastoral administra-
> tor. I don't know if it's saying more than we want it to
> say at this point. On the other hand, there's always a
> need for symbols, and for some official dimension of
> this role. This is someone who has an appointment. So
> I don't know if I'd call it an installation. I guess I'm
> ambivalent about what to have. I think it's important to
> say the bishop is behind the person, but maybe we
> could call it something else, instead of an installation.

A deacon, who was not warmly accepted by some of his
parishioners, said he felt that an installation ceremony would have
helped him because the bishop's presence might have had a stronger
impact on the parishioners. When I asked his bishop if he would
consider installation ceremonies in the future, he said this:

> I'm talking to my priests and other ministers about this.
> Because if this is really something that's going to be

official, then I want it to be done in an official way. I would anticipate that this is going to be the road we will be going to go down in the long haul, and I don't want to give folks the wrong impression. So I want us as a diocese to know that this is the route we're going, so that it becomes a meaningful ministry.

By contrast, another deacon explained his rationale for not requesting an installation ceremony:

I wanted to establish myself. I wanted to kind of earn my own wings here, rather than coming in on the bishop's coattails. But eventually, within a month or so, I did have the bishop down. But it was not for an installment ceremony. It was just to meet the people, but it amounted to the same thing. The symbolism was still there, because I was sitting right there with him at Mass. I was the deacon, read the Gospel, and did all that stuff, sitting right next to him.

Another deacon told me that the installation of nonpriests as parish leaders was not a practice in his diocese. Nonetheless he asked the bishop to install him, and the bishop agreed to come. The parish leader explained that it was he and his parishioners who "put the installation rite together." Reflecting on the bishop's presence at the installation, the deacon said, "I did need the support, because it was not an easy transition."

A married leader described a dramatic moment that took place in the sacristy just before the Mass on the day of his installation:

Everyone was waiting. He [the bishop] was waiting, and I was waiting, and the servers were waiting. The musician was waiting. Everybody was waiting. And the bishop looked at me and said, "When are we going to start?" And I said, "Well, you're the bishop. You tell me." And he said, "But you're the pastor. We're in your church. So you tell me if we're ready to start."

A bishop, who was more cautious about the installation ceremony, expressed his position in this way:

> I don't know that the word should be installation. But I could see some way of presenting that person to the community as the one who would provide a certain level of pastoral leadership in their midst. And whether that's to be called installation or a presentation or an affirmation of their presence, I'm not too sure. I would want to, on the one hand, check out the canonical implications of whatever is done, and on the other hand, the source of encouragement and support to the person who will be working there. It's good for the community to experience that kind of affirmation, but I would want to be clear that the person could not function as a pastor per se, that the person would be a pastoral leader.

Another bishop said he used the occasion of the installation ceremony to give some advice to the children of the parish leaders. He explained,

> I talked to the kids in that installation rite, but I wanted the parish to hear it. So I was really talking to the parish. I said to the kids, "We know you've got to be good, but you don't have to be any better than anyone else. And let me tell you my theory. My theory is everybody should get into a little bit of trouble every single day. Not the kind that hurts anybody. Not the kind that breaks anything. But just the kind that lets people know

you're around. But that means your folks can get into a little bit of trouble, too. And you can't say anything about it." They all laughed, but it was for the parish, and for them as well.

The Bishops' Ongoing Support

When I asked people about the subsequent support of the bishop, their responses revealed a number of decisions and actions on the bishop's part that illustrated his continuing assistance for the new leadership. The following supportive actions emerged from these interviews: evaluation sessions, visiting the parishes, substituting for the visiting priest, benign neglect, inclusion and exclusion, verbal and social support, and economic sustenance.

Several of the dioceses have periodic evaluations of pastoral administrators. For instance, one of the bishops calls a meeting of all parish directors every six weeks or so. He explained, "We get them all together and establish the agenda together from their questions. So I have the chance to evaluate, monitor, and share the journey periodically."

This bishop also told me that in their diocese they use the same process of evaluation that they have in place for the priest pastors of the diocese. He said,

> It was helpful to follow the same procedure and have an assessment meeting for all new pastors, including the nonpriests heading parishes, after the first six months. We do that for all new pastors, and say, "How is the communication going? What's going well? What needs clarification?" We've tried to pull in the parish council to be part of the procedure.

In one diocese the bishop not only established a workshop for new parish leaders, but he also insisted that it be a yearly event. He said,

> I've asked that a small workshop be provided each year on "Parish Director Issues." So that anybody who is either curious or whatever wanted to come to it, it would be available. They did it one year, but they didn't do it another. I said, "I asked you to do this." They said, "Well, we didn't think there was a need." I said, "I think there's a need. Would you please put it on the schedule?"

One bishop went out of his way to welcome the new parish leader and his family. The deacon's wife described it this way:

> The first week that we were here, I'll never forget it. My husband and I took the rental truck back, and we came home and our older son was in the parking lot, and he was jumping up and down. "Mom, mom! The bishop's here!" He had come to welcome us, and was sitting in the living room, talking to our kids. He just dropped in.

Some parishioners were eager to tell me about the day when their two bishops came to visit some farms in their area, and participated in their ice cream social on the front lawn of the church. A male parishioner described this unprecedented visit of the bishops. He said, "When they came down here, I took off work early. The whole town also participated." Prior to the bishops' visit, a female parishioner asked the parish leader what she should call the bishop. He told her that she could call him "Your Excellency" but that he prefers "Bishop." Later she proudly told the parish leader, "I called him 'Father Bishop.'" During our interview the married leader summarized it in this way: "She figured she had covered all her bases that way. So hopefully it will help them to see who [the bishops] are, and that they're real people, and that they're okay."

A lay leader located in a small rural parish in the deep South described an extraordinary show of support by his bishop on two separate occasions: the day of the dedication ceremony for the new parish church and confirmation. He said,

> The bishop, who had a heart attack six weeks earlier, and was not supposed to resume his duties for six weeks, came to our dedication the day after the six-week period was up. He couldn't even drive himself. The chancellor had to drive him. And realizing that he's playing to a house that's two-thirds non-Catholic, he explained why he was putting this garment on, why he was using oil.

A deacon described a visit by the bishop during his first month on the job, when he used the title "pastor":

> [The bishop] came because he wanted to reaffirm my job. And he stood at the lectern, and he said to the people that day, "I want you to understand that you asked for an ordained person, and we brought that to you by means of Deacon….He is your pastor."

A bishop told me that he felt he was fairly visible when he comes to the parish for confirmations, and he mentioned a practice that others might emulate. He said, "I try to take the pastoral administrators out to lunch once a year, just to see how they're doing."

A Hispanic deacon described his bishop as "a great bishop": "He comes for the celebration of Our Lady of Guadalupe every year. And if we need help, he's right here."

By contrast, a parishioner in another parish said,

I'd like to see [the bishop] a little more often. Just for him to show up and say, "I'm going to worship with you all because I enjoy being with you." But I don't want him to just show up for a confirmation or send us a letter three or four times a year asking for some money. I don't appreciate that.

On the other hand, one of the bishops told me that soon after he was assigned to his present diocese, he went through on a series of parish visitations. He described the scope of his activities during each parish visit:

I'd be in a parish for two, three days at a time: visit all the classrooms, visit all the shut-ins, bring communion to the sick, had a Mass with the anointing of the sick, met with all the committees, met with the staff if there is one, had confirmation, maybe. I went through the whole diocese. It took me eight years.

I learned of an extraordinary example of a bishop's support in a parish in a small rural town. The wife of a parish leader reported that her husband often had difficulty in finding priests to substitute for their assisting priest when he was sick or on vacation. She quoted the bishop who surprised her the first time he came to the parish to celebrate Mass in the middle of the week, on a holyday of obligation. In his opening announcement to the people, he said, "I'm a bishop and I come to [the parish church] because you couldn't get anyone else. I'm so glad you couldn't get anybody else, because I had an opportunity to come."

This wife told me that she viewed the bishop's actions as an extraordinary show of support for her parish. She described herself as someone who "doesn't have any great shakes for any of the hierarchy" because of the "pomp and circumstance" aspect. But referring to the bishop's greeting, she announced:

> This is wonderful stuff. This is what people want to hear. They need to see their bishop doing something besides the confirmation routine."

She explained that whenever her husband was unable to find another priest to come to his parish as a substitute for Mass on Sundays, one of the bishops would come. She described the parishioners' reactions: "So they think [my husband] must be like God Almighty if he can get the bishop down here." A visiting priest said this about his bishop:

> [He] has a wonderful sense of benign neglect. He knows just when to step in and more effectively he knows when to let things be. He follows in the tradition of his pred-ecessor here, who described himself as "a Vatican II bishop." Part of [the bishop's] relationship to the pres-byterate was empowerment. If you had a good idea, "You bring it to me and we'll work together"....a lot of letting things happen. Consequently there evolved a really good rapport with the episcopal leadership that we still have here, which is really a key element.

One of the deacons told me that his assisting priest, who was elderly and in poor health at the time, was not able to administer the anointing of the sick to his parishioners at home or in the hospital. In this case, for a period of about three years, the bishop gave the deacon his permission to administer this sacrament.

The deacon explained,

> Of course I would not hear confessions or anything. But I was given the faculty to anoint. It was a hidden

faculty. I don't have it anymore. It was taken away from me.

This unusual action on the part of the bishop could be described as a special concession to the deacon in that situation. It reminded me of the laity who were secretly ordained in Czechoslovakia during the communist regime so that they could administer the sacraments for the spiritual benefit of the people.

One of the married leaders told me about a yearly gathering of priests, originally called "clergy days," that was later renamed "pastoral leaders days" in order to include all of the pastoral administrators on these occasions. He described the meetings as "very supportive":

> Some people say, "Oh, no big deal." To me it was very significant to say that, in a lot of ways, we're all pastoral leaders. Some are priests, some are sisters, some are lay, but we're all pastoral leaders within this church.

A bishop described the strategy he used on an occasion when a married leader was excluded by an older priest during a Holy Thursday chrism Mass at the cathedral. The bishop said,

> The first year that [the married leader] attended the chrism Mass, I saw this out of the corner of my eye, but I was preoccupied in the sacristy. He came into the sacristy with his alb, and I saw the pastor, who is a stickler for the letter of the law, take [the married leader] out. I thought he was taking him to the library where the priests were vesting. I found out afterwards that he told [the married leader] to take his vestments off.
>
> I apologized to [the married leader] when I heard it. I said, "Don't ever take orders from anybody else other than myself. Anytime the priests and deacons are vesting, you ought to be vested as well, and you ought

to be in the procession. Your place is right there with the deacons.

A pastoral administrator who was also the tribal leader in a Native American parish attested to the bishop's encouragement regarding adaptation of their rites. He said that both their own assisting priest and the bishop were encouraging them to make these changes. He explained,

> Christianity plays a very important role in doing away with a lot of rites, our rites that could have been adapted to the Christian faith. We have encouragement from the bishop, but it's not been done....We feel that these rites should be incorporated into Masses. Even though we have had some encouragement from the bishop, some priests are still not doing it, because they don't have the language.

The wife of a parish leader attested to the verbal support of their bishop:

> The bishop really likes [my husband]. I mean, he says "I wish I had a dozen of you." He's very complimentary. The bishop and [my husband] work very well together. The bishop's in a hard spot because some of the priests are very open to [my husband], but there are some who are very threatened.

One of the bishops lauded the "family dimension" of married pastoral leaders:

> There is a family dimension to it that you can't get away from, and I think it helps greatly. I think also their real

respect and mutuality that there is between them has a lot to do with it.

Another bishop echoed these sentiments:

I think that people will and do relate to him because of the fact that he's married and has a family on the grounds that he understands the issues that they're facing. He knows what he's talking about when he talks about children and all.

On the other hand, a wife described a communication between her husband and the bishop that was not supportive. She said her husband had talked with the bishop "a couple of different times about [his assisting priest's] mental problems." When her husband brought the same subject up in a recent telephone conversation, the bishop's reply was, "What can I do? Just pray for him." The wife's reaction was, "Well, that's a big help!"

Another lay leader testified to his bishop's written as well as verbal support:

There was a parishioner who was very upset about the inclusive language, and the fact that we had made some changes in the lectionary, based on an approved translation. This person wrote to the bishop to complain, which is really not that unusual. But the bishop, in a very nice way, wrote a short letter back and basically supported what we were doing at [our parish], and encouraged the person to talk to me if there was any further issue. And it was a very supportive thing.

A married leader expressed these sentiments about his bishop's strengths:

It's his humanity that's probably the biggest support for me. The fact that he will call up and apologize for not seeing me as often as he thinks he should, and ask what he can do for me, or should we meet for dinner or something.

I know I can go in to see him with feelings that you might want to label as, "Oh boy, this is a stupid question." But he's willing to listen and you don't feel intimidated by the fact that he's a bishop. It's just the fact that he's open. So he can be a mentor, and yet he's the bishop.

A married leader explained why he has no need to ask his bishop to "bail him out" when parishioners question his authority:

I know some parish directors have had troubles with parishioners who were members of the parish finance council or other parish groups. So when I came in, I made it very clear that I'm not hired by the parish. I'm appointed by the bishop to do this. So we've never had any miscommunication about who's in charge here. And I've never had to have the bishop come in and do any kind of crisis management.

An African American deacon said this about his bishop:

He's been very supportive of me. There's not anything that I can't approach him about. His door is open. I can pick up a phone at any time of day and call the chancery, and I get right through to him. There's not a "hold" or "I'll get back" or anything like that. So I have a direct access to him, and that's a relationship that he and I have built up over the years. He has a love for me, and I have a great love and admiration for the bishop. And there's not anything that he would ask of me that I wouldn't do, and I think the same thing in reverse is true.

While discussing a very poor parish in his diocese, a bishop remarked that the parish was unable to provide for the parish leader's salary. So, in that case, the diocese picked up his salary. When I asked him if any of the richer parishes adopted the poorer parishes like this one, he replied,

Some of that is happening on an informal basis in this diocese. I would like to see it formalized in the future, because some parishes, like his, may not be hooked up into that. He may not have all the contacts that some of the others have because of their ability to establish those relationships.

However, the parishes in economic need trusted that, in the last analysis, they could count on their bishop for economic sustenance. One of the parishioners in a parish located in a barrio on the edge of the city, gave credit to the bishop for their continuing existence. She stated,

There were talks of closing [our parish] several years ago. We obviously don't bring in enough money, so we're not a very cost-effective place to keep open. But we get the support from the bishop.

A parishioner in an African American parish on the outskirts of a large city attested to the bishop's financial support. She said, "Our parish is completely supported by the diocese, because the parish cannot afford anything by itself. We're not self-sufficient."

The Bishops' Views about the Future

It is not surprising that those bishops who have had a longer experience with the appointment of nonpriest pastors had more to say about the future of such parishes. Some of these bishops, in fact, are viewed as pioneers in the creation of this new type of parish for the Catholic Church. Their insights focused on two topics: continuity and discontinuity and church renewal.

A bishop reflected on parish changes in this way:

> There is a dimension of restructuring in parish leadership, but there is also the dimension of continuity. Because even where there is a nonpriest who is in charge of a parish community, the traditional sacramental ministries are still offered, and many, if not all, of the other aspects of the parish continue to be in place.
>
> So in that sense there isn't a restructuring, but a continuity. The new dimension is the person who provides the pastoral leadership for all of the other non-sacramental celebrations or activities to the life of a parish. And in the absence of a priest, there is a pastoral leader who can provide direction, insight, counseling, and moral guidance when they seek that kind of personal assistance. So the structure of the parish remains pretty much intact, and the sacraments remain intact. The new dimension is the person who is there on a continuous basis.

Another bishop analyzed the pain and discontinuity involved in the closing of parishes:

> The bishops don't want to close parishes, either, but they're forced to do it. And you know, it's very painful, both for the communities involved, and for the bishop.

And there's a lot of bitterness and rancor that has developed, that we all know about.

One bishop said he did not feel comfortable about having pastoral administrators, and he would rather have priests in every parish. To that end, he is strongly recommending prayers for vocations to the priesthood. Likewise another bishop is urging families to be involved in working for priestly vocations. He told me that he would mention people like Cardinal Bernardin to his parishioners, and then pose questions like, "Can't you see that we need to tell kids that that's a wonderful way to live your life? To do the wonderful things that these people have done?" He concluded by stating, "That's what I think we have to do."

By contrast, another bishop pointed to the hiring of alternate parish leaders as a sign of hope for small parishes:

Most of our pastoral administrators are serving in very small parishes that are on the verge of existence or nonexistence. They're at sustenance levels. And I think that probably also makes a big difference in how he is received or not received into the parish. So if [the diocese] is willing to hire somebody like this, it's a sign of hope for the parish.

Yet another bishop spoke of the struggle over priestly identity. He told me that he had just heard that a pastoral administrator had himself listed as the pastor in one of the church bulletins. He explained, "So I had to say gently that doesn't fly. I do think we have to be continually vigilant about the identity question."

A bishop voiced a similar stance:

If we leave a parish without a priest pastor for too long, we've formed the people in a way that I don't think is wise. We're right on the edge of that right now here. We've got to make some changes....It's a priest morale problem. Insecurity is a biggie for priests right now, for any number of reasons. And when you get parish directors who are very charismatic and well-received, and priests who are less than that, that's tough on their morale.

The same bishop quickly added that there was a morale problem among parish directors as well, because "if the priests perceive them as a threat, then it's very hard for them to be accepted in the leadership of the diocese." This is how he described the thoughts and feelings of parish directors:

> They love the priests. They don't want to take their place. They just want to serve the church. They don't feel that they're in competition, but they do feel badly when the priests think they are. So both camps are a little bit insecure.

A parish director spoke glowingly about the parish leaders days held in his diocese, where all leaders, priests and nonordained, meet together. He described it this way:

> We have morning prayer together. Everyone's there who wants to be there, and sings and listens and participates the ways you hope people would, and I just get pumped up. Being together and saying, "Hey, we're all leaders together. We're all in the same boat. This is great."

A bishop gave his rationale for supporting collaborative ministry: "There isn't much energy going on in those parishes where the priest is really elderly, and barely gets over to the church to say Mass." In fact he labeled these parishes as "almost dormant." He stated that a young or middle-aged couple who are practicing collaborative leadership is "much better for the parish," and he labels their energizing influence "the cutting edge of parish leadership." He ended the interview by stating, "In fact, collaborative ministry is our watchword. It has to be collaborative ministry."

A bishop discussed the issue of ordination of married men to the priesthood in the context of church renewal:

> I'm very open to people's ideas and their discussions....I'll listen to their experience. People are saying, "We want Eucharist. Why can't we ordain laymen?" In Latin America we have a parish with eighty lay catechists, men who are leaders of the little communities up in the mountains. And they have communion every day and religious services and Bible studies. And the people say, "Why can't we ordain Juan and have him be our priest?"
>
> The big issue is because he's married. Well, come on. Let's say the issue is because he doesn't have the training. Okay, fine, let's get him the training. Let's provide the training and move on with it.
>
> I just think that there's no stopping the renewal that's taking place. Many believe that we're off in a wrong direction. They're more comfortable with having a static version of theology. This historical, developmental approach to theology gives them the creeps. We still have a revealed religion. But you could certainly listen to the experience of people when they say they wouldn't have any difficulty having ordained priests who are married. So I'm very open to collaboration, and to discussion, and to seeing the difference between those things that are central to our faith and those things that could change.

Another bishop described an incident that convinced him of the latent leadership and goodwill among parishioners. He said there was a time when a priest of his diocese was murdered, and he had to drive down to that parish, knowing that he had no priest to send them. He said,

> Honestly, I didn't know what I was going to tell them. As I'm driving down there, I'm saying "What am I going to tell these people?" This is a parish that was used to having three Masses on Sunday, and the priest was very energetic. And of course it was a shock to the parish.
>
> But the priest had prepared the parishioners for the fact that things were changing in terms of numbers of priests. He had let his people know that there is a shortage, and he had gotten them working in the parish.
>
> When I got down there, the head of the parish council stood up in front of everybody and started out by saying, "Bishop, we're here to find out how we can help you." That sentence hit me like a ton of bricks, and I will never forget that. It was such a relief to hear him say that.
>
> When the death happened, the parish had already appointed all of the committees, and they kept things going, and carried that parish for six months, until something could be done. I'll never forget that. We have a lot of latent leadership, and a lot of goodwill among the parishioners, and we need to draw on that.

The wife of a parish leader described her bishop's view of church renewal and of the future. It contrasted sharply with the preceding statements. When word and communion services were discussed, her bishop said that he favored the Eucharistic services instead. She explained,

> In other words, the bishop favors Mass, like every Catholic does. He thinks every parish deserves to have a Mass on Sundays. His prediction is that there's going to be a tremendous Eucharistic renewal. Now that means he's seeing an increase of priests, because the Eucharist means Mass, and only a priest can say Mass.

Another bishop spoke to the issue of the priest shortage when he said,

> My feeling is that what we're doing now could last for ten years. But if there hasn't been some change in ten years, then I think we have to rethink the whole situation again. Right now we don't have enough assisting priests. That's going to be the major issue: to keep the sacramental dimension going. So we'll get strapped in between five or ten years from now, and then we're going to have to relook at the whole basis upon which we're doing this.

A backlash in some parts of the country that is manifesting itself in a growing clericalism troubled one of the bishops:

> There's a certain amount of reaction against the whole notion of pastoral administrators, and it's growing. There are places where they thought they'd never have pastoral administrators. In [large cities] they thought, "We'll never have to do that because we have all these priests." Well, now we're beginning to see it happen in larger places.
> So now the clericalism starts to pick up. They don't want to appoint someone who's not ordained to

be really in charge. They want the priest supervisor from the next parish, so that gives him effective control, because you can always go beyond the pastoral administrator to the supervisor. So it really in fact makes the supervisor the super pastor.

And then there's the reluctance to give the person who is the parish leader any kind of title that would indicate that person's in charge, so they start calling them "associates." Somehow this whole business of not wanting them to be in charge seems to me a major obstacle.

Summary

There is no doubt that the bishops had some different views about the future of parish life. Imagine the lively conversations we might hear if we could each be a "fly on the wall" as an observer at a gathering of these bishops whose voices we have heard, both in this chapter and throughout the book!

Some bishops were also more organized than others regarding the preparation of parishioners and the screening of candidates for this new position. On the whole, however, due to the supportive actions of the bishops, evidenced by their installation ceremonies, parish visits, evaluation sessions, and their economic support, the deacons and laymen in charge of parishes tended to express their conviction that they could count on the bishops' validation of their leadership.

Chapter 8
Conclusion

All of the central characters in this book were involved in the creation of new roles for a different form of ministry in Roman Catholic parishes. The pioneering efforts of these married parish leaders, their wives and children, their parishioners, priests, and bishops have created a legacy for those who follow in their footsteps. It is my hope that both present and future nontraditional parish leaders will find it easier to move into their new positions because of what they learned from the experiences of others recorded in these pages. There is no need for the future generation to "reinvent the wheel."

Summary

The first chapter introduced the change in church law that allows bishops to appoint persons who are not priests to be in charge of parishes. A summary of previous research on alternate parish leadership was followed by an explanation of the theory and methods of data collection used for this study.

Chapter 2 revealed the limitations on these married leaders in the administering of sacraments. Although deacons had more sacramental authority than laymen, the lay leaders shared their status as laity with their parishioners. But all of these leaders had two important advantages: the same marital status as the majority of their parishioners, and the collaborative leadership that they practiced.

In chapter 3 we met the spouses of these married leaders who were mature, well educated, and enthusiastic supporters of their husbands' new position. Most of them also contributed financial support by working outside the home. In every case their husbands were the first nonpriest in charge of the parish, and the wives invented strategies for either more or less visibility in their new parish role.

The children's reactions to being a "pastor's kid" and the experiences of the families who lived in the rectory were recorded in the fourth chapter. The presence of children helped their father to "break the ice" with parishioners who were apprehensive about this new situation. Though the children disliked being "watched" as the pastor's kid, they were proud of him, and "helped dad out" with part-time jobs.

In chapter 5 we turned to the parishioners, who were mourning the loss of their priest pastor, yet willing to work with their new parish leader to keep their parish open. The collaborative leadership practiced by their parish leaders was the key to success because it gave the parishioners a sense of ownership. One parishioner described his parish as "a mosaic, where every piece counts."

The priests who served as sacramental ministers in these parishes were highlighted in chapter 6. Like all of the other major actors in the previous chapters, the priests found themselves in "uncharted territory." But the added stress of serving as pastors in their own parishes and traveling to another parish (or two) each weekend—the burnout syndrome—is taking its toll on these priests. It was especially painful to hear the eight priests who lived alone describe their bleak living arrangements, devoid of the community that would have been possible with the companionship of fellow priests.

Finally, in chapter 7 we met the bishops who appointed the married men as leaders of these parishes. Some bishops had "done their homework" regarding the preliminary processes: choosing parishes for alternate leadership and preparing the parishioners beforehand. The next phase included processing applications for the job of parish leader, and the screening and selection of candidates. A formal installation ceremony held in the parish church with the bishop as the presider, and his continuing support—verbally, socially, and economically—was an important source of strength for these new parish leaders. In fact, one of them quoted his bishop's words, "You're the pastor."[1]

Implications for Future Research and Policy Changes

What is needed to supplement my in-depth qualitative study focusing on the people "in the trenches" of these twenty parishes is a nation-wide survey of parishes without resident priests that will give us the statistics for a more comprehensive view of nontraditional parishes. This will help us to see how widespread the issues, strategies, and attitudes are regarding the acceptance or nonacceptance of alternate parish leadership. The sample should include parish leaders and (if married) their family members, parishioners, sacramental ministers, and the bishops who appointed the new leaders.

Some implications for changes in policy should also be addressed. At this point in time there are dioceses in the United States that have more than ten years of experience with alternate parish leadership. The guidelines that have been developed in these dioceses should be collected, compiled, and made available so that other dioceses might benefit. What I am recommending is a collection of diocesan documents throughout the country that sets forth the guidelines regarding such processes as the recruitment, selection, and appointment of alternate parish leadership. After these documents are compiled and categorized, they should be made available for other interested parties.

As the priest shortage continues to accelerate, the policy of assigning priests as sacramental ministers is vital to this project, but to assign them to several parishes is an invitation to burnout. As early as 1988, Bishop Raymond Lucker warned:

> We need to face the fact that our priests have been heavily burdened. They cannot continue to add to the number of parish masses to offer, meetings to attend, and programs to be personally involved in.[2]

This bishop, a pioneer in the appointment of pastoral administrators, also voiced this apprehension:

> I'm especially concerned about those priests who are sick, discouraged, worn out and those who are thinking about leaving the active ministry. I see a bleak future with no young men in the major seminary and so few in college seminaries preparing for priesthood.[3]

There is another category of priests, however, who are even more likely to suffer burnout: Those priests who are appointed not only as the pastor of the parish where they reside, but also as the pastor of one or two other parishes where there is no pastoral administrator in residence to perform the various nonsacramental duties. Table 2 in the appendix shows that there were 2,241 parishes in the year 2000 that were served by these circuit-riding priests. Because there is no systematic research on this topic, we can only imagine the degree of strain experienced by these priests without a community living situation who have full responsibility as pastor of the parish where they reside and as pastor to one or sometimes two other parishes as well. Consequently they must spend hours on the road each week to fulfill all of their pastoral duties. A nation-wide research project that focuses on priests who are literally working a "second shift" as pastor is imperative.

Toward a Different Form of Parish Leadership

In order to keep parish communities alive, what is needed are new resources for parish leadership that will re-invigorate the sacramental life in these parishes without priest pastors. This would necessitate a change in church law along the lines of Thomas Sweetser's recommendation, one that is not a new phenomenon, but a return to the practices of early Christianity.

Although they were not priests, the parish leaders in this study not only "kept the parish open" but, following in the footsteps of the apostles like St. Peter, they showed that the married state is not an impediment to church leadership. In fact, their marital status offered two advantages: Their family members provided a community living situation for these parish leaders, while their wives and children contributed to the creation and maintenance of the parish community as well.

The issue of the sexual abuse of minors by Catholic priests in the United States occupied the headlines in the first half of 2002 and is almost certain to be a negative influence on the recruitment of candidates to the priesthood in this country. In addition, the removal from active ministry of hundreds of priests accused of the sexual abuse of minors over the past forty years will exacerbate the shortage of priests for parish ministry.[4] The parishes portrayed in this book are evidence that another form of leadership is not only available, but it also can be instrumental for the healthy continuation of parish life in the United States.

Some bishops have already raised the issue of the ordination of married men. But will it work? Will the parishioners accept married priests? My own experience in twenty parishes headed by married men leads me to predict that it may not be a smooth process in some parishes, especially in the first few months. However, given the parishioners' demand for sacramental services and their commitment to contribute their own time, talent, and monetary resources for the survival of their parishes, this research project suggests that married priests will eventually receive full acceptance as pastors.

My visits to parishes without a resident priest where married deacons and married laymen were in charge enabled me to witness the beginnings of a transformation in the leadership of Roman Catholic parishes. Married parish leaders are no longer a "question" or an "issue," but a reality. In my attempt to uncover a portion of the mysteries of God's creation I was privileged to have a glimpse of the beginnings of a life-giving form of leadership for these parishes. As I near my seventieth year of life, I feel a deep sense of gratitude for this unique opportunity.

Appendix:
The Priest Shortage

Schoenherr and Young's demographic study, *Full Pews and Empty Altars* documented the growing shortage of priests in the United States over a forty-year period beginning in 1965 and projecting to 2005.[1] They predicted a 40 percent reduction in the number of active priests by the year 2005. Over the same time period they predicted that this shortage in the supply of priests would be accompanied by a 65 percent growth in the demand for priestly services resulting from increased membership, and driven by high fertility rates and escalating numbers of Hispanic and Asian immigrants. They argued that a decrease in the supply of priestly services accompanied by an even greater increase in the demand for them would precipitate a major demographic crisis for the Catholic Church in the United States.

For example, Schoenherr and Young predicted that even priest-rich dioceses in the Eastern part of the United States like Boston and New York would begin to feel the effects of the priest shortage by the year 2005. An article in the April 3, 1998 issue of the *National Catholic Reporter* corroborated that prediction.[2] It stated that the development of a pastoral plan to take the Boston archdiocese to its bicentennial in 2008 may require the closing of up to sixty parishes in the next ten years. Although there were 735 active priests in the archdiocese in 1998, the number of priests was projected to shrink to 573 by 2005. The shortage of priests may be even greater in Boston and other Roman Catholic dioceses throughout the United States as a result of the removal from ministry of priests accused of the sexual abuse of minors in the first half of 2002.

What effect has the priest shortage had on parish leadership in the United States?

Froehle and Gautier, researchers at the Center for Applied Research on the Apostolate (CARA) at Georgetown University, report that, as of 1998, "13% of parishes—nearly 2,500 in the United States have no resident pastor."[3]

In addition, Froehle and Gautier report that the growth of the U.S. Catholic population grew from 14 percent of the U.S. population (10,774,989 Catholics) in 1900 to 22 percent (59,156,237) in 1998.[4] At the same time, the supply of priests has been declining since the 1970s. Ordination of diocesan priests, for instance, began a steady decline in the mid-1960s, and between 1965 and 1998 the total number of priests declined from 57,730 to 46,352. In that same period, ordinations declined from 1,575 to 460 per year, while deaths of priests increased from 725 to 1,040 per year, and departures from the priesthood increased from 125 to 230 per year. The highest number of priestly departures (675) took place in 1970, five years after the completion of Vatican II.[5] Froehle and Gautier's research tends to corroborate Schoenherr's earlier findings and projections.

The United States Conference of Catholic Bishops (USCCB) is well aware of the priest shortage. In fact, the most recent study of the priest shortage was initiated in 1998 by Bishop Anthony Pilla, at that time the President of the National Conference of Catholic Bishops. The Bishops' Conference commissioned researchers at CARA to conduct this project, entitled "Study of the Impact of Fewer Priests on the Pastoral Ministry." One part of the study was a survey that included information such as: (1) the actual number, age, and distribution of priests; and (2) current and anticipated pastoral practices for future pastoral ministry in light of the priest shortage. Other sources of data came from focus groups of priests, deacons, and lay ministers, and a random sample telephone survey of Catholic laity. The results of this study were reported in June 2000, by Bishop Richard C.

Hanifen, chairman of the Bishops' Committee on Priestly Life and Ministry.[6] Some of the findings are listed:

1. Over the past forty years the Catholic population has grown in all regions of the United States. The greatest growth was in the West, a 261 percent increase, followed by 196 percent in the South, 59 percent in the Midwest, and 52 percent in the East.

2. Over the past ten years, 82 percent of dioceses report that they do not have enough priests to meet their pastoral needs. The priest shortage is most critical in the Midwest and West, and less so in the Northeast and South. The ratio of priests to people in 1950 was approximately 1:650, and in 1999 it was 1:1200.

3. By 2000 the average age of priests was fifty-seven years for diocesan priests and sixty-three years for religious priests.

4. Sixteen percent of all priests active in parish ministry are immigrants from other countries, in particular Ireland, India, the Philippines, Poland, Vietnam, Mexico, Colombia, and Nigeria.

5. Fifty-eight percent of the dioceses have already appointed nonpriests to head parishes, and 53 percent of the dioceses report that they expect to increase the number of these appointments during the next ten years.

6. Other strategies that have been utilized by dioceses to address the situation of fewer priests are closing parishes (13 percent of the dioceses), and reducing the number of Masses (42 percent).

7. This shortage also impacts on priests and deacons. Because of their growing administrative responsibilities, priests report frustration caused by less time for the fulfilling aspects of their ministry—sacramental and interpersonal relationships. Deacons report that their talents are well utilized in the parish, but they are worried about the increased time spent in sacramental and liturgical ministry, which has an impact on the time spent in their primary ministry: works of charity.

TABLE 2

Administration of
U.S. Roman Catholic Parishes, 2000

TOTAL NUMBER OF PARISHES	19,008	
With resident pastor	15,985	84%
Without resident pastor	3,023	16%
	19,008	100%

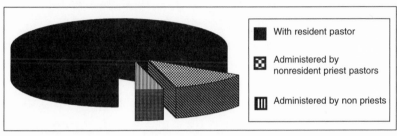

Legend:
- With resident pastor
- Administered by nonresident priest pastors
- Administered by non priests

PARISHES WITHOUT RESIDENT PASTORS
ADMINISTERED BY:

Nonresident priest pastors	2,241	74%
Resident nonpriests	782	26%
	3,023	100%
Parishes administered by:		
Deacons	114	15%
Brothers	18	2%
Sisters	296	38%
Laity	313	40%
Teams	41	5%
	782	100%

Source: Data from *The Official Catholic Directory*
(New Providence, N.J.: Kenedy, 2001)

Table 2 is an update on our national situation regarding alternate forms of parish leadership.

The largest slice of the pie chart in Table 2 represents the proportion of parishes in the United States that had a resident priest pastor in 2000, 84 percent or 15,985 of the total 19,008 parishes in the United States. The remaining 16 percent or 3,023 parishes that did not have a resident priest are represented by the checked and striped portions of the pie. The checked portion, 74 percent (2,241) represents the parishes administered by nonresident priest pastors, and the striped portion, 26 percent (782) represents the parishes administered by nonpriests, the focus of this book.

The statistical breakdowns at the bottom of Table 2 indicate some important decisions made by dioceses. When a diocese reaches the point when not enough priests are available for assignment as pastors of parishes, the first alternative in most dioceses in the United States is to entrust the parish to a nonresident priest. Table 2 shows that by 2000 the largest portion, 74 percent or 2,241 of these parishes without a resident priest, depends on a priest who travels to one or more parishes to perform his pastoral duties on the weekend. Some of these priests have experienced the "burnout syndrome" that I discussed in chapter 6 on the priest's role as sacramental minister in these parishes.

The breakdowns by alternate leadership type at the bottom of Table 2 reveal that in 2000 the laity (married and single laymen and laywomen) exercised the largest portion of alternate parish leadership, 40 percent (313), closely followed by sisters, at 38 percent (296). Deacons contributed 15 percent (114) of the leadership, followed by teams at 5 percent (41), and brothers at 2 percent (18).[7] Since religious sisters and brothers are not ordained, and therefore are not clergy, another way of analyzing these data is to compare lay and clerical parish leaders. Adding the numbers of sisters and brothers (314) to the laity category, doubles the percentage of laity heading parishes without resident priest pastors in 2000, bringing the laity's share to 80 percent (627).

How do the results shown in Table 2 on the administration of Catholic parishes in 2000 compare with earlier time frames? Table 3 shows the number and percentage of Catholic parishes in the United States without resident pastors administered by nonpriests

TABLE 3

Administration of
U.S. Parishes without Resident Pastors by
Alternate Leadership Types: 1990, 1995, 2000

Administered by:	1990		1995		2000		Change: 1990–2000 Number:	Percent Change:
Deacons	42	18%	74	21%	114	15%	72	171%
Brothers	21	9%	10	3%	18	2%	-3	-14%
Sisters	145	61%	187	53%	296	38%	151	104%
Laity	24	10%	58	16%	313	40%	289	1204%
Teams	4	2%	26	7%	41	5%	37	925%
Total	236	100%	355	100%	782	100%	546	231%

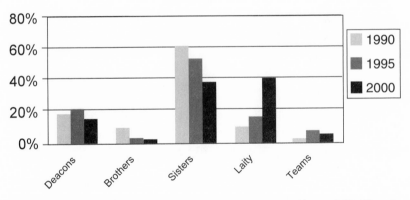

Source: Data from *The Official Catholic Directory* (New Providence, N.J.: Kenedy, 1991, 1996, 2001)

over a ten-year period. In 1990 the total number of parishes with alternate leadership was 236. By 1995, it increased to 355, and by 2000, there were 782 parishes with alternate leadership. This means that from 1990 to 2000, the total number of parishes with alternate leadership more than tripled, from 236 to 782.

Table 3 also depicts the changes in leadership type in U.S. parishes without priest pastors over a ten-year period. The increases in number and percentage of parishes with these leadership types is instructive. However, parishes administered by brothers decreased slightly from 21 in 1990 to 18 in 2000, while parishes with the other leadership types increased dramatically. Parishes administered by sisters more than doubled, from 145 to 296, while parishes administered by deacons nearly tripled, from 42 to 114. In addition, parishes administered by laity increased more than tenfold, from 24 to 313.

The decrease in numbers of sisters and brothers can be partially explained by the continuing decrease in religious vocations since 1965. Froehle and Gautier have documented the changes from 1965 to 1998, showing that the number of sisters in the United States declined by 52 percent and brothers declined by 54 percent.[8]

It is important, however, to keep all of these data on parishes without resident priests in perspective. By 2000 the total number of Catholic parishes in the United States was 19,008, and the 782 parishes with alternate leadership represented only 4 percent of the total number of parishes. The numbers of new parish leaders have not reached major proportions in the United States at this point in time, but their continuing increase has been consistent since 1965, and there are no signs of a reversal of these trends. In fact the dismissal of priests involved in sexual abuse of minors will increase the need for new forms of parish leadership.

How does our national data on the administration of Roman Catholic parishes compare with the global situation? There has been a continuing increase in the numbers of parishes that are administered by deacons, brothers, sisters, and laity throughout the world. Provost, citing data from the 1993 *Annuarium Statisticum Ecclesiae (Statistical Yearbook of the Church)*, reported that at that time there were 3,162 parishes throughout the world that were headed by nonpriests (deacons, religious sisters and brothers, and lay persons).[9] Comparing these more recent data with the situation in 1973, when there were 1,046 such parishes,

TABLE 4

Administration of Roman Catholic Parishes Worldwide, 1999

TOTAL NUMBER OF PARISHES	215,368	
With resident pastor	161,861	75%
Without resident pastor	53,507	25%
	215,368	100%

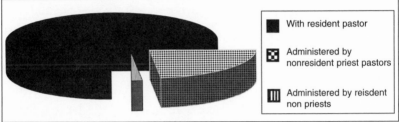

	With resident pastor
	Administered by nonresident priest pastors
	Administered by reisdent non priests

PARISHES WITHOUT RESIDENT PASTORS
ADMINISTERED BY:

Nonresident priest pastors	50,158	94%
Resident nonpriests	3,349	6%
	53,507	100%

Parishes administered by:		
Deacons	576	17%
Brothers	204	6%
Sisters	967	29%
Laity	1,602	48%
	3,349	100%

Source: Data from *Annuarium Statisticum Ecclesiae* (1999)

Provost makes the point that although representing only 1.5 percent of the parishes worldwide, this is a 33 percent increase over the twenty-year period from 1973 to 1993.

Table 4 is an update of Provost's analysis, from the 1999 *Annuarium Statisticum Ecclesiae* (*Statistical Yearbook of the Church*), the most current published international data available at the time of this writing. The number of parishes entrusted to nonpriests by 1999 was 3,349.

A comparison of Roman Catholic parishes worldwide in Table 4 with parishes in the United States in Table 2 reveal similarities and differences in the following situations: (1) parishes with resident priest pastors, (2) parishes where the pastor is a nonresident priest, and (3) parishes with alternate leadership (deacons, brothers, sisters, laity). First, the parish leadership in the United States has a higher percentage (84 percent) of resident priest pastors compared to 75 percent worldwide. Second, the worldwide proportion of parishes without resident priests that are administered by a nonresident priest is 94 percent (50,158), compared to 74 percent (2,241) in the United States. Third, with regard to alternate leadership types in parishes, the pattern of choosing alternative leadership are the same in the United States and worldwide: Laity are the first choice, followed by sisters, deacons, and brothers.

However, there are four important differences in the percentage of these new forms of parish leadership: (1) More use of laity as parish leaders worldwide (48 percent) than in the United States (40 percent), (2) The United States has more parishes where sisters are in charge (38 percent) than parishes worldwide (29 percent), (3) Parishes with deacons as parish leaders is slightly higher around the world (17 percent) than in the United States (15 percent), and (4) Parishes entrusted to brothers are barely visible in the United States (2 percent), even less than they are worldwide (6 percent). The USCCB study, in fact, shows that the number of religious brothers has been dwindling since 1966, from the peak of approximately 23,000 in 1966 to 17,000 in 1998.

Notes

Foreword

1. Subsequently published in a bilingual English-Spanish edition by the National Conference of Catholic Bishops as *Sunday Celebrations in the Absence of a Priest* (1994).

2. Albany: State University of New York Press, 1992.

Chapter 1

1. See Ruth A. Wallace, *They Call Her Pastor: A New Role for Catholic Women* (Albany: State University of New York Press, 1992).

2. See Canon 517.2, *Code of Canon Law: Latin-English Edition* (Washington, D.C.: Canon Law Society of America, 1999). For a longer discussion of the impact of the documents of Vatican II that led to these changes in church law, see *They Call Her Pastor*, pp. 2–8.

3. See James A. Coriden, *The Parish in Catholic Tradition: History, Theology and Canon Law* (New York/Mahwah, N.J.: Paulist Press, 1997), p. 61.

4. Ibid., pp. 66–67.

5. Walter M. Abbott, *The Documents of Vatican II* (New York: America Press, 1966).

6. Schoenherr and Young's research on the priest shortage in the United States led them to predict that by the year 2005 there would be a 40 percent loss of diocesan priests. They also predicted that there would be a 65 percent increase in the demand for priestly services, due to a continuing increase in church membership caused by high fertility rates and the increased immigration of Latino and Asian immigrants. See Richard A. Schoenherr and Lawrence A. Young, *Full Pews and Empty Altars: Demographics of the Priest Shortage in United States Catholic Dioceses* (Madison: University of Wisconsin Press, 1993). For an update on the consequences of the priest shortage, see the Appendix in this book. It

provides more recent data on the priest shortage and on the changes in the administration of Roman Catholic parishes that have taken place between 1990 and 2000.

7. See Joseph H. Fichter, S.J., *Wives of Catholic Clergy* (Kansas City, Mo., Sheed & Ward, 1992), p. 100.

8. Ibid., p. 99. See also Virginia Stillwell, *Priestless Parishes: The Baptized Leading the Baptized* (Allen, Tex.: Thomas More Publishing, 2002). This work is based on interviews with eleven lay parish leaders and four diocesan coordinators in the United States.

9. Cusack and Sullivan's 1995 book on applications of canon 517.2 defining the roles, qualifications, and procedures for parishes entrusted to non-priests is an important handbook for parishes with alternate forms of leadership. See Barbara Ann Cusack and Therese Guerin Sullivan, *Pastoral Care in Parishes without a Pastor* (Washington, D.C.: Canon Law Society of America, 1995).

10. The summer research grant was funded by the George Washington University Facilitating Fund.

11. See William V. D'Antonio, James D. Davidson, Dean R. Hoge, and Ruth A. Wallace, *Laity: American and Catholic: Transforming the Church* (Kansas City, Mo.: Sheed & Ward, 1996), p. 126; and William V. D'Antonio, James D. Davidson, Dean R. Hoge, and Katherine Meyer, *American Catholics: Gender, Generation, and Commitment* (Walnut Creek, Calif.: AltaMira Press, 2001), p. 109; and *Los Angeles Times*, "Los Angeles Times Survey of Roman Catholic Priests and Nuns in the United States," February 20–22, 1994.

12. See D'Antonio et al., *Laity: American and Catholic*, p. 126.

13. See D'Antonio et al., *American Catholics*, p. 106.

14. *The Official Catholic Directory* (New Providence, N.J.: Kenedy, 1996).

15. A friend of mine sent a church bulletin from a parish where a semi-retired priest lives in a house across the street from the rectory. Under the heading "parish staff" the church bulletin listed the name of one of the sisters living in the parish rectory as "Parish Life Coordinator (Pastor)," followed by the name of the priest, who was listed as "Parish Moderator (semi-retired)."

16. See Jay P. Dolan ed., *The American Catholic Parish: Volume II: The Pacific, Intermountain West and Midwest States* (New York/Mahwah, N.J.: Paulist Press, 1987).

17. Ibid., p. 374.

18. Two of the parish leaders were childless, and six of them had children who were married and living in distant towns or away at college.

Chapter 2

1. The mean age was 50.65 and the median was 51.

2. See Bryan T. Froehle and Mary L. Gautier, *Catholicism USA: A Portrait of the Catholic Church in the United States* (Maryknoll, N.Y.: Orbis Books, 2000), p. 112.

3. See *They Call Her Pastor*, p. 13.

4. Although my sample of parish leaders was not a random sample, and therefore cannot be generalized to the Catholic population as a whole, this profile is similar to the Catholic population in the United States, which is 78 percent white, 16 percent Hispanic, 3 percent African American, 2 percent Asian, and 1 percent Native American. See *Catholicism USA*, p. 16.

5. Ibid., p. 142.

6. The alb is a full-length white linen vestment with long sleeves, gathered at the waist with a cincture, that is worn by the priest officiating during Mass and the sacraments. The alb is also worn by a deacon when he is assisting the priest, and is sometimes worn by laity on such occasions.

7. See *They Call Her Pastor*, p. 75.

8. See Patricia Hill Collins, *Black Feminist Thought: Knowledge, Consciousness, and the Politics of Empowerment* (Boston: Unwin Hyman, 1990), 247, for a discussion of her concept "outsiders within."

9. See Patrick H. McNamara, *Called to be Stewards: Bringing New Life to Catholic Parishes* (Collegeville, Minn.: The Liturgical Press, 2003).

Chapter 3

1. See Erving Goffman, *The Presentation of Self in Everyday Life* (Garden City, N.Y.: Doubleday, 1959).

2. See Doris Kearns Goodwin, *No Ordinary Time* (New York: Simon & Schuster, 1994).

3. A similar situation occurred in my earlier study of women heading Catholic parishes. When the manuscript for my book, *They Call Her Pastor*, was in the proofing stage, one of the women pastors informed me that she had been terminated "because the bishop found a priest." Since she was a member of a religious community, however, she also had an important "cushion": the option of living with her sisters in one of their convents while she searched for another job.

4. See *Wives of Catholic Clergy*, pp. 100 and 106.

5. As I mentioned earlier, strictly speaking, religious sisters and brothers are also laity, because they are not ordained.

Chapter 4

1. Pseudonyms are used throughout.

2. See *The Presentation of Self in Everyday Life*, pp. 22–30 and 122–40.

Chapter 6

1. *They Call Her Pastor*, p. 138.

2. For an excellent analysis of the issues involved in the use of these guidelines by parishes without resident priests, see Kathleen Hughes, R.S.C.J., "Sunday Worship in the Absence of a Priest: Some Disquieting Reflections" *New Theology Review* 8 (1995): 45–57.

3. See Table 3 on the administration of U.S. parishes without resident pastors in the Appendix.

4. See "Des Moines Task Force Planning for Parish Development" *Origins* 26.17 (October 10, 1996): 263.

Chapter 7

1. See a discussion of canon 517.2 in chapter 1.

Chapter 8

1. Thomas P. Sweetser, S.J., also uses the term "pastor" when referring to non-ordained persons who function as the resident pastor. See Thomas P. Sweetser, S.J., *The Parish as Covenant: A Call to Pastoral Partnership* (Franklin, Wis.: Sheed & Ward, 2001), xiv. Sweetser recommends that parishes shift to a "pastoral partnership" consisting of "the priest pastor and at least one other person" that provides for "a dual focus of leadership." Sweetser states, "This change of system makes sense not only for the present situation but if and when the underlying culture of the institutional Church changes and returns to an ordained priesthood that includes both married and celibate candidates." See p. 13.

2. See Bishop Raymond A. Lucker, *My Experience: Reflections on Pastoring* (Kansas City, Mo.: Sheed & Ward, 1988), 20.

3. Ibid., pp. 42–43.

4. Alan Cooperman and Lena H. Sun, "Hundreds of Priests Removed Since '60s." *The Washington Post* 9 June 2002, pp. 1 and 18. This article was a report of a nationwide survey of Latin Rite Roman Catholic dioceses in the United States, with ninety-six of the one hundred seventy-eight dioceses responding.

Appendix

1. *Full Pews and Empty Altars*, pp. 57 and 297–99. See also Schoenherr's second book on this topic, entitled *Goodbye Father: The Celibate Male Priesthood and the Future of the Catholic Church*, ed. David A. Yamane (New York: Oxford University Press, 2002).

2. See "Parish Closings Predicted," *National Catholic Reporter*, 3 April 1998, p. 7.

3. See *Catholicism USA*, , p. 121.

4. Ibid., p. 3.

5. Ibid., p. 117.

6. See Bishop Richard C. Hanifen, "Study of the Impact of Fewer Priests on the Pastoral Ministry," www.usccb.org/plm/studyifp.htm, p. 1, viewed on January 15, 2002. This survey, sent to U.S. diocesan offices, had a return rate of 100 percent from diocesan priests and 89 percent from priests who were members of religious orders. These are astounding rates of return for social science survey research, as 60 percent is the norm, and 70 percent or more is unusual.

7. *Teams* is a term that means a group consisting of a priest with lay men and women, and sometimes a deacon, who take turns traveling to a group of parishes for weekly liturgical and other sacramental duties. A team can also mean a group of priests who administer several parishes. For that reason it is difficult to categorize teams as either clergy or lay.

8. See *Catholicism USA*, p. 128.

9. See James H. Provost, *In Diversitate Unitas: Monsignor W. Onclin Chair* (Leuven, Belgium: Uitgeverij Peeters, 1997), pp. 48–49.

Bibliography

Abbott, Walter M., S.J., ed. *The Documents of Vatican II*. New York: America Press, 1966.

Annuarium Statisticum Ecclesiae (Statistical Yearbook of the Church). Vatican City: Libreria Editrice Vaticana, 1999.

Berger, Peter L., and Thomas Luckmann. *The Social Construction of Reality*. New York: Doubleday, 1966.

Code of Canon Law (Latin-English Edition). Washington, D.C.: Canon Law Society of America, 1999.

Collins, Patricia Hill. *Black Feminist Thought: Knowledge, Consciousness, and the Politics of Empowerment*. Boston, Mass.: Unwin Hyman. 1990.

Coriden, James A. *The Parish in Catholic Tradition: History, Theology and Canon Law*. New York/Mahwah, N.J.: Paulist Press, 1997.

Cusack, Barbara Ann, and Therese Guerin Sullivan. *Pastoral Care in Parishes without a Pastor*. Washington, D.C.: Canon Law Society of America, 1995.

D'Antonio, William V., James D. Davidson, Dean R. Hoge, and Katherine Meyer. *American Catholics: Gender, Generation, and Commitment*. Walnut Creek, Calif.: AltaMira Press, 2001.

D'Antonio, William V., James D. Davidson, Dean R. Hoge, and Ruth A. Wallace. *Laity: American and Catholic: Transforming the Church*. Kansas City, Mo.: Sheed & Ward, 1996.

Dolan, Jay P., ed. *The American Catholic Parish: Volume II: The Pacific, Intermountain West and Midwest States*. New York/Mahwah, N.J.: Paulist Press, 1987.

Dolan, Jay P., R. Scott Appleby, and Debra Campbell. *Transforming Parish Ministry: The Changing Roles of Catholic Clergy, Laity, and Women Religious*. New York: Crossroads, 1989.

Fichter, Joseph H., S.J. *The Pastoral Provisions: Married Catholic Priests*. Kansas City, Mo.. Sheed & Ward, 1989.

————.*Wives of Catholic Clergy*. Kansas City, Mo.: Sheed & Ward, 1992.

Froehle, Bryan T., and Mary L. Gautier. *Catholicism USA: A Portrait of the Catholic Church in the United States*. Maryknoll, N.Y.: Orbis Books, 2000.

Gilmour, Peter. *The Emerging Pastor: Non-Ordained Catholic Pastors*. Kansas City, Mo.: Sheed &Ward, 1986.

Goffman, Erving. *The Presentation of Self in Everyday Life*. Garden City, N.Y.: Doubleday, 1959.

Goodwin, Doris Kearns. *No Ordinary Time*. New York: Simon & Schuster, 1994.

Hughes, Kathleen. "Sunday Worship in the Absence of a Priest: Some Disquieting Reflections." *New Theology Review* 8 (1995): 45–57.

Lucker, Raymond A. *My Experience: Reflections on Pastoring*. Kansas City, Mo.: Sheed & Ward, 1988.

McNamara, Patrick H. *Called to be Stewards: Bringing New Life to Catholic Parishes*. Collegeville, Minn.: The Liturgical Press, 2003.

Murnion, Philip, and David DeLambo. *Parishes and Parish Ministries*. New York: National Pastoral Life Center, 1999.

Official Catholic Directory, The, 1991, 1996, and 2001. New Providence, N.J.: Kenedy.

Provost, James H. "Temporary Replacements or New Forms of Ministry: Lay Persons with Pastoral Care of Parishes," in *In Diversitate Unitas: Monsignor W. Onclin Chair*. Leuven, Belgium: Uitgeverij Peeters, 1997.

Renken, John A. "Canonical Issues in the Pastoral Care of Parishes without Pastors." *The Jurist* 47 (1987): 506–19.

Schoenherr, Richard A. *Goodbye Father: The Celibate Male Priesthood and the Future of the Catholic Church*. David A. Yamane, ed. New York: Oxford University Press, 2002.

Schoenherr, Richard A., and Lawrence A. Young. *Full Pews and Empty Altars: Demographics of the Priest Shortage in United States Catholic Dioceses*. Madison: University of Wisconsin Press, 1993.

Stillwell, Virginia. *Priestless Parishes: The Baptized Leading the Baptized*. Allen, Tex.: Thomas More, 2002.

Sweetser, Thomas P., S.J. *The Parish as Covenant: A Call to Pastoral Partnership*. Franklin, Wis.: Sheed & Ward, 2001.

Wallace, Ruth A. *They Call Her Pastor: A New Role for Catholic Women*. Albany: State University of New York Press, 1992.

Index